Ethiopia

Ben Parker
with Abraham Woldegiorgis

Oxfam

© Oxfam GB 1995, 2003

First published by Oxfam UK and Ireland in 1995 (0 85598 270 5)

Revised edition published by Oxfam GB, 2003 (0 85598 484 8)

Oxfam GB is a registered charity, no. 202 918, and is a member of Oxfam International.

ISBN 9 780855 984847

A catalogue record for this publication is available from the British Library.

Reprinted by Practical Action Publishing
27a Albert Street, Rugby, CV21 2SG, Warwickshire, UKz
www.practicalactionpublishing.org

Since 1974, Practical Action Publishing has published and disseminated books and information in support of international development work throughout the world. Practical Action Publishing is a trading name of Practical Action Publishing Ltd (Company Reg. No. 1159018), the wholly owned publishing company of Practical Action. Practical Action Publishing trades only in support of its parent charity objectives and any profits are covenanted back to Practical Action (Charity Reg. No. 247257, Group VAT Registration No. 880 9924 76).

Series designed by
Richard Morris, Stonesfield Design.
This title designed by Richard Morris.
Typeset in FF Scala and Gill Sans.

Cover designed by
Rowie Christopher

This book converted to digital file in 2010

Ethiopia
Breaking New Ground

JENNY MATTHEWS/OXFAM

Ben Parker
with Abraham Woldegiorgis

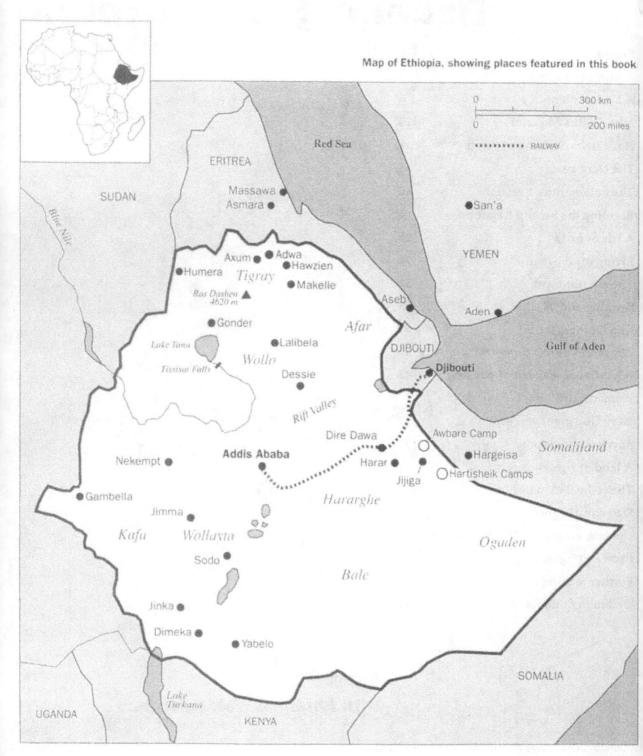

Map of Ethiopia, showing places featured in this book

Beginnings

The cradle of humanity

We all come from Ethiopia. Four million years ago, this land was the home of the ancestors of *homo sapiens*. In 1974, near the Gona river in the Afar desert, archaeologists discovered a partial female skeleton which added dramatic new evidence to the story of human evolution. She was called Dinqenesh ('You Are Amazing') by Ethiopians, and Lucy by Dr Donald Johanson, who discovered her. Her Latin name is *Australopithecus afarensis*.

More discoveries in 1994 supported the theory that our earliest ancestors – the first hominids to walk on two legs and evolve away from the apes – were born along the African Rift Valley, which passes through Ethiopia, and continues southwards to Mozambique. Fragments of bone and teeth in the Afar desert of Ethiopia give a glimpse into the dimmest distant past, long before our ancestors used stone tools or fire, and migrated out into Asia and Europe. History is alive in Ethiopia.

Breaking new ground

For the last 3,000 years, a rich and unique culture has been evolving in Ethiopia. In the last 30 years, the land has had to contend with war, famine, and utter destitution. Medieval churches, hewn out of the rock, served as shelters from MiG fighter-bombers. At least half a million people died of hunger. Now an impoverished and battered nation is emerging into an uncertain future with new borders, young leaders, and a radical new political strategy. An uneasy peace prevails, as a new social and economic order takes shape. The stakes are high. Keeping body and soul together is still the challenge for most Ethiopians.

A bird's eye view

As big as France and Spain combined, Ethiopia is home to about 54 million people. In the heart of the Horn of Africa, it is on the borders between the Arab and the African worlds. About half the population is Christian and half Muslim.

The landscape varies from barren, salty desert to lush, dripping forest. Some parts of the Afar desert, in the north-east, are 100 metres below sea level. They seethe with volcanic activity, a moonscape of sulphurous salt pans and rocky lava fields.

Rising westwards beyond the Afar desert, the land becomes higher, greener, and cooler, up to the craggy highlands, where plateaux are riven by gorges and watered by great rivers. The Blue Nile starts its long journey to the Mediterranean at Lake Tana, just below the Simien mountains, where the highest peaks are topped by Ras Dashen (4,620 metres), Ethiopia's highest mountain. The great waterfalls of Tissisat ('water that smokes') at the source of the Blue Nile were described as 'one of the most magnificent, stupendous sights in the creation' by the eighteenth-century Scottish traveller James Bruce. Dividing the highlands from north-east to south-west is the Rift Valley: a vast geological phenomenon that stretches from Syria to Mozambique.

Highland areas are intensively cultivated. Crops are grown wherever possible, on terraced slopes and plateau-tops.

MIKE GOLDWATER/OXFAM

4

To the west of the highlands are forests; to the south-east, rangelands on the border with Somalia; in the far west are fertile arable plains on the border with Sudan. To the north and east is Eritrea, with its 1,000 km coastline along the Red Sea. To the south is Kenya.

At the centre of Ethiopia the capital, Addis Ababa, is the national crossroads. Major roads fan out to the four points of the compass. A 781 km railway leads from Addis Ababa to the Red Sea port of Djibouti.

Ethiopia's million square kilometres include a rich variety of climatic and ecological conditions. Population density ranges from fewer than five people per square kilometre in the herding rangelands of the Ogaden to 200 or more in the central and south-western areas. Most of the population, human and animal, is concentrated in the cool central highlands, settled for more than 5,000 years. Here pressure on land and other natural resources is increasing.

Ethiopia's ecosystems support thousands of species of plants, birds, and mammals; some are found nowhere else in the world, and nine of the mammal species are classified as threatened. Ethiopia is among the most important reservoirs of biological diversity in Africa, and many crops cultivated elsewhere, like millet, are thought to have their genetic origins here.

Above: **a lowland landscape in the Ogaden region**

Below: **Addis Ababa, a city of four million people**

5

A land of plenty

Ethiopia was settled by peoples from two of the main lineages of human ancestry: the Hamitic peoples and the Semitic peoples (named after Ham and Shem, sons of Noah). A third line, the Cushitic ethnic groups, is found particularly in the south and south-west. There are now at least 64 languages spoken in Ethiopia, and perhaps 80 different ethnic groups. The two largest are the Oromo and the Amhara peoples. Other large ethnic groups include ethnic Somalis, Tigrayans, and Gurages. Some of them are spread over national borders, so not all are Ethiopian citizens.

Ethiopia, Cush, Nubia, and other ancient African civilisations merge into each other in translations of Old Testament scripture, travellers' tales, and myths. 'Ethiopia' – mentioned several times in the Bible and in Greek literature

Mural at Axum: the meeting of the Queen of Sheba ('Makeda') and King Solomon

– became a metaphor for remoteness, or plenty, or simply a land of unknown dark-skinned peoples. The name 'Ethiopia' derives from the Greek for 'burnt faces'. 'Abyssinia', as Ethiopia was commonly known by outsiders until the mid-twentieth century, probably derives from the word which Ethiopians use to describe themselves: *habesha*.

The Ethiopians' national literary epic, the *Kebra Negast*, tells the story of the Queen of Sheba travelling from Ethiopia to meet King Solomon of the Jews in Israel almost 1,000 years before Christ. She then returned to Ethiopia and bore a son, Menelik I, from whom Ethiopian Emperors used to claim descent. This rich brew of myth and fable makes the actual early history of present-day Ethiopia almost impossible to trace. But from the last 2,000 years, parts of Ethiopia can

offer a history, with artifacts, recorded events, and travellers' accounts.

When did 'Ethiopia' come into existence, and where was it? Can it be called one of the most ancient states in the world, or is it just an ancient name? Many Ethiopians are proud that the name of their country and its settlements are scattered in the most ancient of historical documents. Others suspect that history has been manipulated to serve the interests of those in power, and that most of the territories of today's Ethiopia bear little, if any, relation to the ancient civilisations of the Red Sea.

The empire of Axum

Ethiopia's natural wealth and strategic location led at the time of Christ to the rise of an important Red Sea trading and military empire, with its capital at Axum in present-day Tigray. The ancient civilisations of northern Ethiopia dominated the Red Sea region for almost a thousand years from 200 BC. A naval power developed, and Axum's traders and travellers, using the port of Adulis on the Red Sea, reached as far abroad as Egypt, India, and China. Exporting ivory, rhinoceros horn, and spices, and importing metal and cloth, Axum grew wealthy and powerful through trade and conquest.

Today, Axum is most famous for its archaeological ruins: obelisks, tombs, and palaces, and the claim by the Orthodox Church that Axum is the resting place of the Ark of the Covenant – the chest containing the ten commandments engraved on stone and handed to Moses by God.

Axum's tallest standing obelisk, 23 metres high, probably a huge gravestone, is carved from a single piece of rock. With windows and doors on ten 'storeys', it looks like the world's first skyscraper. With half a dozen others, it has remained standing through the centuries and withstood the rumbling of tanks and shelling during the Italian invasion of 1935 and the civil war of the 1970s and 1980s.

JENNY MATTHEWS/OXFAM

Axum's tallest standing obelisk, probably marking a grave: 23 metres high, it has windows and doors on ten 'storeys'

Lalibela: built by angels

Christianity was introduced into Ethiopia in AD 341. In the Middle Ages the Orthodox Church built hundreds of rock-hewn churches. The greatest are found near the village of Roha in the Wollo region of the central highlands. Beginning in the twelfth century, workmen and priest-kings constructed a fantastical complex of churches, monasteries, baptismal pools, and secret tunnels. Ethiopian legend says that the whole massive undertaking was inspired by a dream of King Lalibela, and built with the help of angels.

The churches are almost invisible until one stumbles upon them through an ordinary-looking Ethiopian town. Carved into the hillside, each of the ten churches is interconnected by a series of labyrinthine passages, stairways, and openings carved in the red rock.

On a cool Sunday morning, the austere chants of some of the 450 priests of Lalibela rise echoing from the subterranean places of worship. Deep drum beats resonate from the recesses of the churches. Worshippers from the town and surrounding villages kneel to kiss the rock itself and, wrapped against the cold in traditional thick, white, *gabi* blankets, murmur prayers to the walls.

Skeletons of famous monks are still stored in crevices in the rocks. Inside the gloom of the churches, frayed embroideries shroud the inner sanctum from prying eyes and tourists' cameras. Sunlight pierces the open windows in shafts, and pigeons flutter noisily in the courtyards. Indian swastikas and Jewish Stars of David are carved side by side on the walls, striking evidence of Ethiopia's position at the crossroads of human beliefs.

The movable monarchy

After the almost monastic period of King Lalibela, dynasties came and went, capitals rose and fell, and power shifted from the northern Tigrayans to the central Amharas and back. Society oscillated between anarchy and feudal monarchy, closely associated with the Orthodox Church. Literature and philosophy flourished. There was no fixed capital, but the seat of power was effectively wherever the king and his army happened to be camped.

Islam had filtered into Ethiopia from Arabia since the time of the Prophet Mohammed, and its strongholds were naturally towards the east of Ethiopia. From the mercantile city of Harar, Ahmed Ibn Ibrahim El Ghazi, nicknamed *Gragn* ('The Left-Handed'), rose up against the Christian emperor Lebna Dengel in 1527. Gragn launched a *jihad* against the Christians, and over-ran much of the country, burning churches and looting gold wherever he went. His armies, demanding conversion to Islam or death, reached as far north as Axum. But travellers' tales of Ethiopia's Christian Empire had filtered out to Europe. In response to Lebna Dengel's appeal, the Portuguese sent a group of musketeers, who contributed to the defeat and death of Gragn in 1543.

Lalibela: a twelfth-century complex of Christian churches, carved out of red rock

JENNY MATTHEWS/OXFAM

8

The coming of the Oromo

At about the same time as the Christian Empire was under attack from the east, the south was being overtaken by the Oromo people. They spread north, east, and west throughout the sixteenth century, and penetrated the Amhara areas as far north as Wollo and Gojjam. Gragn's former power base, Harar itself, was attacked until a peace agreement was signed in 1568. The Oromo region today makes up the heart of Ethiopia. The conquests and subsequent settlement of Oromos all over Ethiopia have been described by one sociologist as 'the making of modern Ethiopian society'. Rather than ruling the people of the areas they invaded, the Oromo tended to integrate and intermarry. Today, they are the most numerous ethnic group in Ethiopia, and one of the largest tribes in Africa.

The rise and fall of the Empire of Gonder

As Ethiopia recovered, reduced in power and territory after 16 years of civil war, the Emperors moved farther north and west, close to Lake Tana. A new capital was formed at Gonder in 1636, which became the first fixed capital of Ethiopia since Lalibela. A series of rulers built solid palaces and castles in the city, and some finely decorated churches still stand testimony to the zenith of Ethiopia's renaissance.

The Gonderine empire itself began to collapse in the late 1700s, and Ethiopia disintegrated into an amalgamation of principalities controlled by warlords. From the mid-nineteenth century, two unifying leaders, Tewodros II and Yohannes IV, started to pull Ethiopia together again.

Enter the British

Tewodros II tried to gain support for his reforms and technical schemes by writing to Queen Victoria. When his letters went unanswered, he imprisoned a British consul and several missionaries. This led to a British military expedition, which stormed his mountain stronghold at Magdala in 1868, where Tewodros, crying 'I shall never fall into the hands of the enemy', shot himself in the mouth with his pistol. The British force then proceeded to loot the libraries of the palace and church nearby, taking hundreds of manuscripts back to England. Few have been returned from the British Museum to this day.

Yohannes IV, a chief from Tigray, succeeded in holding the expansionist forces of both Egypt and Italy at bay, but was killed in battle against the Sudanese Mahdist armies in 1889. Power then reverted to the Amhara line, from the central region of Shoa, and Emperor Menelik II was crowned.

Imperial monument in Addis Ababa: the black-maned lion is the symbol of Ethiopia's dynasty of emperors, who claimed descent from King Solomon

JENNY MATTHEWS/OXFAM

Menelik the Moderniser

Emperor Menelik II was a moderniser and an expansionist. In a series of brutal raids on neighbouring peoples, he tripled the territory of the empire. But he also managed to withstand the European 'Scramble for Africa', through a combination of cunning and brute force. He imported modern firearms in large numbers, and understood the rivalries that motivated the Western powers as they used Africa as a playing field for their power struggles.

The Italian government had its eye on Ethiopia, from the vantage point of its colony in Eritrea. In 1895, the Italians invaded Tigray, in northern Ethiopia, and occupied the town of Adigrat. Menelik assembled an army of 100,000 troops and moved north to challenge them. When the decisive battle took place, near Adwa, on 1 March 1896, the Italians were outnumbered by about five to one, and outmanoeuvred. This humiliating defeat of a white army in Africa, according to Ethiopian historian Bahru Zewde, 'stemmed the tide of colonialism'. It also led to treaties that established Ethiopia's newly-expanded borders, which have more or less survived until the present.

The symbolic and historical significance of the battle of Adwa, which preserved Ethiopia's independence until the 1930s, is one of the most potent ingredients of Ethiopia's special status in African and black history.

During Menelik's reign, Ethiopia saw the advent of motor cars, Ethiopic typewriters, piped water, the telegraph and the telephone, and diplomatic relations with foreign powers. With the support of his wife Empress Taytu, a leader in her own right, he established the foundations of a modern state: a bank, a post office, a railway line to the port of Djibouti, and schools and hospitals.

While modernising the centre, Menelik terrorised the periphery. The bitter experiences of peoples such as the Gurage, the Wollayta, the Kafa, the Beni Shangul and the Gimira, who suffered terrible and brutal conquest, still rankle today. Tens of thousands of people from newly conquered regions in the south-west were sold to be slaves of the highlanders. Only in September 1923 did Ethiopia ban the slave trade.

Menelik II is the most controversial figure in modern Ethiopian history. Ethiopia owes its borders to his conquests, and also perhaps owes him its instability and ethnic disharmony. In trying to cement together a huge mosaic of peoples, he was storing up trouble for his own successors. He left behind a chaotic struggle for succession, and a country that had expanded but not consolidated its new territories. Kingdoms and principalities, especially among the Oromo lands, on the verge of statehood themselves, were unceremoniously annexed, and forced to pay tribute to the Ethiopian Emperor. Menelik's successes in technological progress have to be set against the turbulent legacy which his 'African colonialism' left behind.

Haile Selassie, King of Kings

As Emperor Menelik's health declined, there was a bitter struggle for power, from which Ras Tafari Mekonnen emerged as the King of Kings in 1928. His coronation in November 1930 was a spectacular pageant, designed to reinforce Tafari's legitimacy as the heir to the Solomonic line, and to put Ethiopia on the map internationally. Ras Tafari Mekonnen took the name Haile Selassie, which means Power of the Trinity. His full title was His Imperial Majesty Emperor Haile Selassie, King of Kings, Conquering Lion of the Tribe of Judah. Kings, diplomats, and journalists were invited from all over the world to take part in the festivities, so beginning an era in which unprecedented numbers of foreigners were to visit Ethiopia, and Ethiopians of the elite were to travel abroad for education and entertainment.

Haile Selassie, during a fifty-year reign, tried to reform and modernise Ethiopia, but, at home, was finally overtaken by the expectations which his limited reforms generated. His foreign policy, at least, inspired Africans and people of African descent all over the world.

Ethiopia was among the first of the developing countries to join the League of Nations (formed after the First World War to ensure peace and collective security). Admitted to the club in 1923, on condition of the abolition of slavery, Ethiopia was soon to find that all nations were not equal in the League, and that a weak country without friends or influence abroad could be abandoned without so much as a murmur.

The Italian invasion

Fascist dictator Benito Mussolini and the Italian army, still bitter about the defeat at Adwa in 1896, saw Ethiopia as the natural extension of the coastal colony they had established in 1885 and named Eritrea. Haile Selassie saw that the invasion was inevitable. Although he managed to buy arms from Western powers, he obtained no promises of support from them.

The Italian invasion from Eritrea began on 3 October 1935, at the same time as an attack from the south-east, from Italian Somaliland. The Ethiopian barefoot army was no match for the Italians' modern forces, supported by armour and air power. The Italians were ruthless in their suppression of civilians. Mustard gas was sprayed on rural communities, in contravention of the Geneva Convention, causing terror and agonising death. The Emperor fled to England days before the fall of Addis Ababa, on 5 May 1936. He spent the rest of the war in Bath, agitating for the liberation of Ethiopia. But Britain and France, some historians believe, initially allowed Mussolini a free rein in Ethiopia, in a vain attempt to appease his African ambitions, and keep him out of an alliance with Hitler.

The Italian invasion and occupation of Ethiopia was brutal and totalitarian. Laws tantamount to apartheid were enacted, and brutal retribution was inflicted on civilians after any act of resistance. Mussolini's military commander is reported to have promised to deliver Ethiopia 'with or without the Ethiopians', and was as ruthless as he promised. At Debre Libanos monastery, several hundred monks were executed on suspicion of helping the resistance. A row of skulls and boxes of bones near a cave in the cliffs are still on show.

Having routed the Axis forces in North Africa, the British army supported the Ethiopian resistance fighters, who defeated the Italians in 1941. After an uneasy period of cohabitation between the Emperor and the British authorities, who seemed unwilling to restore power to Haile Selassie, eventually the Emperor gained an unconditional return to power, and the inclusion of Eritrea and the Ogaden within Ethiopia's territory.

The remains of the Italian occupation can be seen most impressively in the Ethiopian road system: stunning switchback passes in the mountains and long straight highways driven through the Ogaden desert. The coffee bars of the capital and the Italian jargon of car mechanics are reminders of the brief but influential Italian period.

Post-war Ethiopia

It is hard to say when the Second World War ended for Ethiopia. Only in 1954 did it regain all the territories that it had controlled before the Italian invasion.

Unwilling to be left without a powerful military ally again, and ambivalent about the British, Haile Selassie entered into a close post-war alliance with the United States. By the time of the 1974 revolution, Ethiopia was receiving about 60 per cent of all US military aid to Africa, and large amounts of development aid.

Haile Selassie used the post-war period as a chance to develop his armed forces, but also to invest in education, social reform, commerce, and agriculture. His downfall came about because he never dealt decisively with the underlying problems of landlessness, political monopolies, and regional alienation.

The Emperor ruled autocratically (his divine right to rule ratified by the 1931 and 1955 constitutions), but encouraged the development of an intelligentsia. He promulgated constitutions and created a parliament, but gave it no real power. He made token appointments of Oromos and other classes usually not included in the ruling elite, but did little to encourage genuine equality. Women's legal rights as parents were not established until the 1955 constitution.

Haile Selassie I University, later renamed Addis Ababa University, was established as an African centre of learning for students from the entire continent

The Derg years

The 1974 revolution

Political change has rarely, probably never, come about by peaceful means in Ethiopia. As early as 1943, a rebellion in Tigray had been put down with the help of British aircraft from Aden. Army officers challenged Haile Selassie in a military coup that failed in 1960. There was an Oromo uprising in Bale in the 1960s. War with Eritrean rebels fighting for independence had been going on for 12 years already, when in late 1973 student demonstrations and strikes broke out in Addis Ababa. Struggling against a severe drought and impending famine, farmers in the countryside refused to pay their feudal landlords' tax demands. A BBC documentary film of a famine in the northern Wollo region during 1974, edited together with shots of Haile Selassie feeding titbits to his favourite lap dog, caused outrage in Addis Ababa.

The Imperial Navy mutinied in February 1974, and the 'creeping coup' continued until a council of military officers, calling themselves the Derg, or 'Committee', elected from the ranks of the armed forces, arrested Haile Selassie on 12 September 1974. The self-proclaimed 225th descendant of King Solomon and the Queen of Sheba was taken away in a Volkswagen Beetle. The Emperor, by then a frail 82 years old, was imprisoned in the old Gibbi palace in Addis Ababa, where he died of suffocation nearly a year later.

The Red Terror

The early years of the Ethiopian revolution were heady ones. University and high school students who had rallied against the failures of the old regime were eager to convert the rural masses to scientific socialism. 40,000 young people

'In Ethiopia they have established very radical measures. In a feudal country, where the peasants were slaves, they have nationalised the land and distributed it among the peasants. They carried out an urban reform, prohibiting any family's having more than one house. ... They organised the families living in poor urban areas. They nationalised the principal industries of the country, revolutionised the armed forces, politicised the soldiers, and set up Political Committees.'

(Fidel Castro, March 1977)

took part in the *Zamacha* ('campaign' in Amharic), teaching literacy and building schools and clinics in the countryside. Land, foreign businesses, and church properties were nationalised in the early stages of the Derg regime. A series of sweeping reforms affected every part of Ethiopian life and destroyed the feudal system completely.

But by 1977 the politicisation of the army had turned the Ethiopian revolution into just another military coup. Idealistic dreams faded as purges, torture, and witch-hunts against political opponents in the cities turned into a meaningless bloodbath. This 'Red Terror' lasted throughout the late 1970s, and conservative estimates from the human rights group Africa Watch say that up to 30,000 people were killed.

Lieutenant Colonel Mengistu Haile Mariam, the son of a night-watchman, clawed his way to the top of the Derg in a series of brutal power struggles. He became Chairman in 1977, at the height of the Red Terror.

Above: **Images of Mengistu the dictator loom over a May Day Parade, Addis Ababa 1988**

The Derg never managed to reach a peace agreement with the Eritrean rebels. It also failed to tackle demands for greater regional autonomy for Tigray, Oromo, and Somali areas. Several armed resistance movements were formed, the most important of which were the Tigray People's Liberation Front (TPLF) and the Oromo Liberation Front (OLF).

The Somali Republic, which had always wanted to unite the ethnic Somali people within its own borders, launched its army against Ethiopia in 1977 in support of the Western Somali Liberation Front, the Ethiopian Somalis' armed faction. The Ethiopian army was pushed back to the highlands, but Somali forces finally retreated in the face of Ethiopian reinforcements, spearheaded by Cuban soldiers, and supplied by the USSR.

Saved by the USSR and Cuba from defeat in 1978, Ethiopia remained firmly in the communist camp for the rest of the Cold War. Socialist central planning of the economy was introduced, and a restrictive agricultural policy gave little incentive to Ethiopian farmers. Price controls and interference in marketing led to mediocre production of food and cash crops.

Ethiopia became the People's Democratic Republic of Ethiopia, controlled by a single party, the Workers' Party of Ethiopia. Open political dissent was dangerous, and rare. Large numbers of political prisoners were detained, and a powerful security apparatus silenced all but a few critics. Tight control was maintained over the media: among the banned books were the Gospel of St Mark and Shakespeare's *Hamlet*.

Right: **Monument to the Revolution, Addis Ababa. The stylised presentation of Ethiopian peasants reveals the influence of Soviet Socialist art.**

14

The famine of 1984/85

The terrible famine of 1984 and 1985 was the result of a combination of war and drought. Early warnings were ignored or mistrusted, and by the time the outside world and the Ethiopian government had been shocked into action by TV reports, it would be too late to save the lives of at least half a million people. The famine marked a turning point for Ethiopia, and for the international community. Ethiopia may never shake off the association with hunger, and the aid organisations and donor governments may never again underestimate the power of public concern to raise money for disaster relief. Goaded by the singer Bob Geldof, the British public alone raised £100 million in response to the famine.

The civil war

Brutalised by a ferocious but incompetent leadership, 100,000 soldiers of the Revolutionary Army died in the civil war that ravaged Ethiopia throughout the 1980s. The former rebel movements are still reluctant to release full details of deaths on their side, but, in Eritrea and Ethiopia combined, their losses were possibly almost as high.

Civilians suffered on both sides of the front lines. In the government-held areas, forced conscription and arbitrary taxation devastated communities, and in liberated areas the Ethiopian Air Force bombed and burnt schools, clinics, and villages in an attempt to terrify people into resisting the rebels. Napalm and cluster bombs were used on civilian targets. Hundreds of thousands of Tigrayans and Eritreans fled from war and drought and became refugees in Sudan. Ethiopians with money or education managed to get refugee status in Northern countries: a brain drain from which the nation is still recovering.

In the most notorious atrocity of the war, a key market town in Tigray, Hawzien, was bombed by Mengistu's air force in June 1988. As MiG bombers pounded the town, helicopter gunships strafed thousands of fleeing civilians. At least 1,800 people died in a single day.

January 1985: The long trek to Sudan begins for people from Abi Adi, fleeing drought and war in Tigray

The nationalities question

Ethiopia has changed shape many times during its long history. The convulsive years of the Derg widened the cracks in the State's relationship with Eritrea until ultimately the northern region broke away completely. Two other regions and peoples – the Oromo and the Somali – threaten to detach themselves from 'Greater Ethiopia'. Their grievances, and the way they are represented politically in future, will have far-reaching implications for the future shape of Ethiopia, and even for its very survival.

Independence for Eritrea

Eritrea was part of the area known to Ethiopians as *Mareb Melash*, until Italy named it *Eritrea*, from the ancient Greek for 'Red Sea'. Parts of today's Eritrea were first occupied by the Ottoman Turks in 1572, and then by the Egyptians. The Italians ruled Eritrea from 1885 until their defeat in 1941 during World War II.

During this period, Eritrea became (compared with Ethiopia) industrialised. A skilled workforce produced goods and foodstuffs for export to Europe and the Middle East. While glad to be free of fascist rule, the Eritreans, accustomed to a separate identity, had mixed feelings about joining Haile Selassie's Ethiopia. At the end of the war, the Allies passed the problem over to the United Nations, which decided in December 1950 to recommend federation with Ethiopia. This compromise pleased no one. The Emperor eventually dissolved the federation, and Eritrea came under direct control from Addis Ababa in 1962.

Ethiopia's repressive measures in Eritrea strengthened rather than suppressed national feeling. Political activity was banned; trade unions were abolished; local languages were suppressed. Resentment against Addis Ababa developed into a full-scale war.

Asmara, the capital of Eritrea, benefited from investment in industry and public services during 55 years of Italian colonisation

Some Ethiopians bitterly resent Eritrean nationalism, claiming that Eritrea is part of Ethiopia's historic heartland, and its people are so closely related to northern Ethiopians as to be identical. This may be true, and Eritrea's sense of national identity was perhaps born of occupation by other countries and cultures. But Eritreans *feel* different, and thirty years of war only reinforced this.

The Eritrean liberation fronts were for many years plagued by religious and ethnic division and rivalry, but one group rose to become the dominant force and finally claimed victory and independence. The Eritrean People's Liberation Front (EPLF), officially formed in 1973, became a disciplined and formidable organisation, with military, political, and social sections administering the majority of the territory which they had gained.

Asmara, the main town in Eritrea, finally fell to the EPLF in May 1991. The Provisional Government of Eritrea, established by the EPLF, held a referendum on independence in April 1993, which produced a 98 per cent vote in favour of leaving Ethiopia. The EPLF dissolved itself in 1994, and within the government of Eritrea it is now the dominant political party, renamed the People's Front for Democracy and Justice. A new constitution is being written.

Ethiopia and Eritrea will always be closely linked, and economic and cultural ties are as strong as ever. But the legacy of bitterness will take generations to fade. And Eritrea's independence has weakened Ethiopia strategically, since Ethiopia is now a land-locked country.

A share of power for the Oromo

Ethiopia's largest ethnic group, the Oromo, live in territory that spreads across central Ethiopia between Sudan to the west, Kenya to the south, and Somalia in the east. The Oromo areas, especially in the west of Ethiopia, are among the richest and greenest in the country. Their agricultural land is the backbone of the Ethiopian economy, yet they have been devalued by rulers of every complexion, and their aspirations have been ignored ever since their incorporation into the empire. Their sheer strength of numbers, and the areas they live in, mean that if Oromia were to secede from the rest of the country, the map of Ethiopia would look like a series of ink spots on the page.

The Oromo, then mainly nomadic herders, began to migrate into today's Ethiopia in the fifteenth century. Some Oromo nationalists claim that they have roots in their current territory going much further back than that. In general, Oromos, despite the ferocity of their initial campaigns, were settlers, rather than tyrants. Some studies suggest there may now be as many as 19 distinguishable 'clans' of the Oromo, each of which has adopted customs, languages, or agricultural techniques from the original inhabitants of the area where they now live. In religion too, Oromos are divided into Christians, Muslims, and adherents of the traditional worship of natural spirits whose God is known as *Waq*.

Oromos had never been excluded from holding token positions of power: some of Haile Selassie's most faithful lieutenants were Oromo. But the Emperor, as in Eritrea, tried to enforce his language, culture, and religion in every region, thereby storing up resentment and allowing no expression of ethnic pride except violence. Children were forced to learn a foreign language (Amharic) at school and often had to change their Oromo names for something which the Amhara teachers could remember easily.

The Oromo Liberation Front, like the Tigray People's Liberation Front, was formed soon after the 1974 revolution. It has now withdrawn from the government, and the Oromo people are represented by a new party, the Oromo People's Democratic Organisation (OPDO). If the OPDO cannot meet the aspirations of the Oromo for greater recognition and better representation in politics and society, Ethiopia's present fragile peace is unlikely to hold.

Secession for the Somalis?

About 2.5 million ethnic Somalis form the second-largest region, after Oromia, in the new federal Ethiopia. The area identifies with Somalia, to which it looks for all of its needs in business, trade, and culture. The region's historical links to Ethiopia are tenuous at best, and the impetus towards secession – either as an independent state, or through unification with the Somali Republic – is strong. The discovery of natural gas in the area makes it strategically important for the Ethiopian central government.

Most Somalis are herders; their nomadic way of life depends on the seasonal migration routes which follow the natural cycles. Invisible borders mean nothing in the desert. The Somalis are now divided among five countries, as a result of the colonial period and Menelik's Ethiopian Empire. The flag of the Somali Republic has a five-pointed star to represent them: Somaliland, Djibouti, Ethiopia, north-eastern Kenya, and the Somali Republic.

The economy of the Somali regions, in whichever country, depends on grazing and water for livestock. When the rains have been good, water in seasonal rivers and wells is plentiful, and resources are shared among the different clans of the Somali people freely. When resources are scarce, tensions rise.

The clans are families which can trace their ancestry to one of the original immigrants from Arabia who settled in present-day Somalia. Children are taught the litany of their ancestors' names, reaching back a dozen generations into history, at their mother's knee. This organisation of society on the basis of ancestry is mixed with a unique form of Sunni Islam – liberal, poetic, and mystical. Decisions are traditionally made by a *shir*, or council of 'elders'. In fact, age has little to do with membership of the council, but gender does. Any grown man can take part in discussion, but women are usually excluded.

Ethiopian Somalis have gained little from being part of Ethiopia, and, if the

A Somali family on the move: all their possessions are packed on the camel

Somali Republic had not been in turmoil at the overthrow of Mengistu in 1991, moves towards separation from Ethiopia might have gathered more momentum. Government forces and secessionist groups in the Ogaden have clashed sporadically for years.

Ethiopia needs to offer Somalis something to make staying within the nation worthwhile. With hardly a road, a telephone, a school, or a clinic to show for fifty years in the 'great Ethiopian family', it will be a key challenge for Ethiopia's new breed of politicians to convince Somalis of the benefits of staying with Ethiopia.

A new voice for Tigray

Just as the Derg failed to resolve the Eritrean question, it could not solve Ethiopia's internal problems. The struggle of regions with different cultures, languages, and customs for greater autonomy was intensified by the overthrow of Haile Selassie. To some, the Derg represented the continuation of repressive central control by one ethnic group, the Amhara. Power had passed between the Amhara and the Tigrayans for generations, but the Amhara seemed to have become entrenched.

The victory of the Tigray People's Liberation Front (TPLF) in 1991 was the culmination of decades of northern resistance to the authorities in Addis Ababa. A rebel group formed in 1975 with just 11 rifles went from strength to strength, fighting until 1991 – not for independence, but for the overthrow of Mengistu's Derg and a new political system.

The TPLF, the EPLF, and the Derg they both fought against were all, officially, Marxist-Leninist. For Western powers, taking sides in a contest between communists was an unappealing prospect, so they remained on the sidelines. But the faultlines of the Ethiopian conflict were much older and deeper than political ideology.

The TPLF made a break with the past in their strategy. Instead of living off the land, as armies had always done, making

people fear them like plagues of locusts, they concentrated on winning hearts and minds in the areas they began to control. Decision-making involved public meetings, which all were encouraged (and sometimes compelled) to attend. Self-reliance and equality between men and women were the new values, and, after centuries of feudalism, Tigrayans supported a movement that listened to them and, literally, spoke their language.

As in Eritrea, the harder Mengistu tried to batter Tigray into submission, the more determined the people became, and young men and women volunteered to fight in the TPLF in their thousands. Morale was high; discipline and political control were rigid, beneath a relaxed

Lete Birhan, 34, was a fighter with the TPLF. Her leg was amputated after she was hit by a tank shell in a battle for the town of Axum, in 1988.

JENNY MATTHEWS/OXFAM

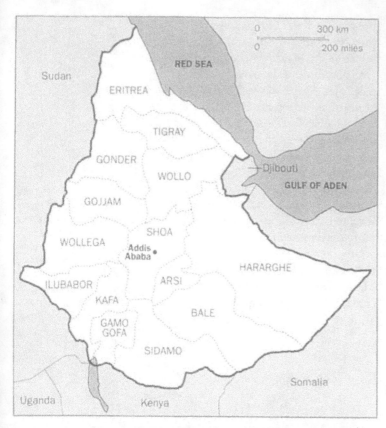

Above: **Traditional regional boundaries of Ethiopia**
Below: **New regional boundaries drawn up by the Transitional Government**

exterior. The TPLF hid in caves and could melt into the rugged scenery during the day, when the MiG fighter-bombers came on patrol. The former rebels claim not to have received external support for their war, and to have captured their weapons from the enemy; but certainly the Eritrean rebels gave the Tigrayans a helping hand to open another front against the Derg.

Life in the war zones, which by the end of 1990 included most of the north of the country, was terrifying and bizarre. Markets were held at night, to avoid bombing raids by day. Farmers even ploughed by moonlight. People passed through military checkpoints with secret messages folded under their tongues, ready to swallow if challenged. And the sounds of war became as familiar as a cock crowing.

A federal system for Ethiopia

On its advance on Addis Ababa, the TPLF was joined by sister movements representing other Ethiopian ethnic groups: Amharas from Gonder, Gojjam, and Wollo had their own movement, the Ethiopian People's Democratic Movement (EPDM). In 1989, a multi-ethnic coalition was formed: the Ethiopian People's Revolutionary Democratic Front (EPRDF). The outlines of the EPRDF's future political strategy began to emerge. The 'nationalities question' – how to bring harmony to a multi-ethnic country with a history of oppression and discrimination – was to be settled by a federal system. Most radical of all, regions were to be allowed to leave Ethiopia if they wanted to, without bloodshed.

In a manifesto printed just before the fall of Mengistu, the EPRDF noted that the break-up of Ethiopia through peaceful regional secession would be 'a lesser evil compared with the present condition of fratricidal war and unmitigated destruction'.

Building the Second Republic

The enigma of the EPRDF

Meles Zenawi, leader of the EPRDF and the TPLF, claimed in an interview with *The Independent* in November 1989 that 'the nearest any country comes to being socialist as far as we are concerned is Albania'. This caused incredulity among many educated Ethiopians and foreign observers. Just as the Berlin Wall was falling, the party which was poised to take over Ethiopia was seeking inspiration from one of the most notoriously repressive and unproductive Stalinist states in Eastern Europe.

But when the rebels arrived in Addis Ababa, the EPRDF, pressurised by Western powers, especially the USA, committed itself to political reform and economic structural adjustment on lines applauded by the World Bank and the International Monetary Fund. The story of the EPRDF's military progress on the road to Addis Ababa is relatively simple. But the development of their ideas, the pressures they were under to adapt their philosophy as the Communist bloc crumbled, and the final U-turn in political orientation are harder to decipher. While retaining the zeal of 'revolutionary democracy' that sustained them as a liberation front, the EPRDF as a political party have shown themselves to be supremely pragmatic – or opportunistic.

The Transitional Government

The EPRDF moved into Addis Ababa on 28 May 1991, re-established order in the cities, and disarmed and dispersed the defeated revolutionary army, with the help of the Red Cross.

A national conference on Peace and Democracy was held in July 1991, to which most opposition groups were invited, with the exception of some political organisations based abroad. The conference established an 87-seat Council of Representatives, in which the EPRDF coalition itself held 32 seats. A national charter guaranteeing the establishment of human rights and democracy was adopted to serve as a temporary constitution, and a programme was laid out for regional and national elections.

The monument to Karl Marx outside the university in Addis Ababa: one of the few communist symbols not to have been demolished since the end of the civil war

JENNY MATTHEWS/OXFAM

Elections in June 1992 established councils to manage the affairs of the regional 'states'. The elections were marred by inadequate preparation, intimidation, and boycotts. The EPRDF and its affiliates swept the board.

The Oromo Liberation Front (OLF), the second-largest party in the national Council of Representatives, withdrew just before the poll; alleging violence, intimidation, and vote-rigging, the OLF returned to military struggle. There was sporadic warfare between forces of the EPRDF and OLF through the rest of 1992, especially in the east. About 20,000 alleged OLF members and supporters were detained by the Transitional Government, only released after months of 're-education' in military-style camps. Skirmishes still continue between the OLF and EPRDF, but in military terms the OLF appears critically weakened, and many of its political leaders are in exile.

It was an unusual first step for a victorious army to volunteer to share power, but in fact expulsions and boycotts by other parties left the EPRDF in effective control of the government for the transitional period.

The adoption of a new Constitution of Ethiopia in December 1994, and elections scheduled for May 1995 for the national legislature – the Council of People's Representatives – mark the end of the transitional period. Meanwhile, the new Constitution has enshrined the right of self-determination for individual peoples, and a series of sweeping proclamations has established new regional boundaries along ethnic lines, and relative autonomy for the regional administrations.

However, the law on rural land holding is one of the most far-reaching constitutional provisions, as Ethiopia's second republic approaches. The law provides for State and communal ownership of land and natural resources, with individual ownership limited to the fruits of the individual's labour. This law is not unlike the Derg's policy on land, both in language and content.

A comprehensive census of population and housing, undertaken in October 1994, will provide much-needed baseline statistics for planning infrastructure and services. The importance of the census for economic planning cannot be over-stated. The currently estimated national

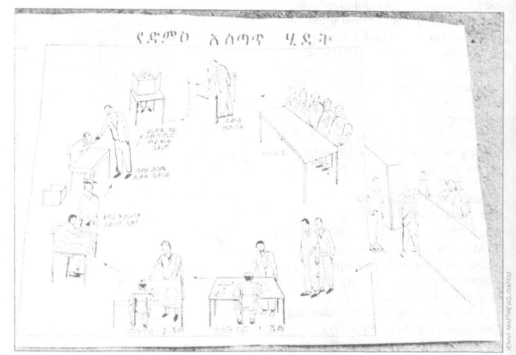

A poster showing the voting process for local elections, Amhara region, 1994

population of 54 million is derived from the 1984 census, excluding Eritrea, and assuming an annual growth rate of 2.9 per cent. The 1984 census, the first in Ethiopia's history, must be treated with caution, because it was conducted during the civil war, when large areas of the country were inaccessible to enumerators.

The aftermath of conflict

Three decades of war and famine in Ethiopia have left millions of broken lives, maimed bodies, and mass graves. Many people are still picking up the pieces of their lives, and the future is uncertain.

Lete Birhan, 34, was a fighter with the TPLF, the spearhead of the victorious EPRDF forces. She was hit in the leg by a tank shell in Axum in 1988 during a battle for the town. 'I could still feel it when they took me to the hospital,' she says, but in the end the doctors had to amputate. She's now a seamstress, retrained with about 1,000 others, mostly younger than her, at a centre run by a government commission for rehabilitating ex-soldiers. 'All of them are youngsters,' says Tadesse Berhe, General Manager of the centre. A graph on the wall in his office shows the terrible toll of injuries to young people in the war: his trainees are grouped according to their disability: blind, one eye, partially sighted, one leg (261 people), spinal injuries, head injuries.

Lete is proud of her contribution to the struggle: at least she can console herself with victory. She chose to join the TPLF, with the blessing of her family, and spent nine years in the field. She doesn't know where she will end up: it depends on where the commission will send her.

Hundreds of thousands of soldiers fought against Lete Birhan's forces after only one month's training. Imru Ile was woken up in his bed in 1988, beaten with sticks and taken off to join Mengistu's revolutionary army. For three years he was stationed in besieged Asmara, now capital of independent Eritrea. Ever since the battle for Asmara, he has had a bullet

JENNY MATTHEWS/OXFAM

lodged in his head. The Red Cross brought him back to Wollayta, and kept him going with food distributions for a few months. Now he is destitute. He has a house, but not even a few pots and pans to cook with. His wife recently died of tuberculosis, when five months pregnant, and he and his tiny daughter Mimi, who is severely malnourished, are living in a nutrition centre.

The flotsam and jetsam of the war turn up all over the country. The largest army in Sub-Saharan Africa, 350,000 men, was demobilised in a matter of months; soldiers were sent home with only a few months' rations to tide them over. Women and children who lived at the barracks were evicted. Three years on, groups of unemployed ex-soldiers still stand around in tattered uniforms all day

Tailoring workshop for disabled war veterans, Adigrat, Tigray region

All over Ethiopia, the rusting debris of war lies scattered along the roads

JENNY MATTHEWS/OXFAM

outside churches in Addis Ababa, playing flutes and begging.

The war at its peak cost US$500,000 a day. Weapons poured into the country, mainly from the Soviet Union. Lives were cheap because guns were cheap, and minor local disputes became more dangerous.

Peace has never lasted long in Ethiopia's recent history. Fifty million people, mobilised for war, and subjected to a barrage of propaganda from all sides, will not settle down quietly into a model nation-state. Almost any Ethiopian you meet has memories: someone in the family was sacked, imprisoned, killed, or became a refugee during the civil war. As a result, optimism is a scarce commodity, and people lead their lives in Ethiopia looking over their shoulders.

Crimes against humanity

The architects of the reign of terror and oppression which led to the death or disappearance of tens of thousands of people during the Red Terror in the late 1970s are now being held to account for their crimes against humanity.

In December 1994, 66 former Derg officials, including Colonel Mengistu Haile Mariam and 20 officials *in absentia*, were put on trial, facing a charge of genocide, in addition to crimes against humanity. In all, 3,400 Derg officials will be charged with human-rights violations in a process which will probably take years.

The grim irony of the trials is that the systematic genocide of the Derg years was well documented in minutes of meetings, taped interrogations, video film, and official orders, all filed by meticulous bureaucrats. The archives also cover the murders of Emperor Haile Selassie and the patriarch of the Ethiopian Orthodox Church, His Holiness Abuna Theophulos.

The Ethiopian trials are the first instance of an African government holding a former regime accountable for its crimes. It is hoped that the 'due process of the law' will help to heal the bitterness of the recent past, and in turn engender faith in a truly democratic second republic in Ethiopia.

Refugees

In the 1980s, when Ethiopia was a watchword for suffering and starvation to the outside world, for over half a million refugees from Somalia and southern Sudan it was a safe haven.

President Mengistu of Ethiopia supported the rebels of the Sudan People's Liberation Army against the Sudanese government, and Sudan supported Mengistu's rebels, the TPLF and the EPLF. President Siad Barre of Somalia attacked Ethiopia, and Ethiopia fought back by supporting four different rebel movements during the civil war in Somalia. The terrible symmetry of Cold War alliances produced a zone of refugee camps in the Horn of Africa, some of which are now permanent towns.

Hawa Ahmed arrived in Hartisheik, Ethiopia's refugee metropolis, in 1988 from her village west of the Somaliland capital, Hargeisa. She came with her husband and five children. Two children died in Ethiopia; her husband was wounded in the leg during the bombing of north-western Somalia, and has not been able to work since. They live in a *buhl*, a large igloo-shaped house typical of the nomadic areas, but in Hartisheik the structure is patched with food-aid bags and bits of cardboard from old boxes of nutritional biscuits. The war with Siad Barre is over, but she still has not gone back. 'We plan to go back: we have some land in Somaliland,' she says. 'The rations here are not enough.'

Hartisheik camp could once have qualified as the second-biggest city in Ethiopia, housing about 250,000 people. The water consumption alone was about 1.2 million litres a day. Water, food, and medicine had to be trucked into the area in an immense relief operation. The

Displaced Somalis building a *buhl* at Awbare (Teferi Ber) camp, eastern Ethiopia, 1994

JENNY MATTHEWS/OXFAM

Happy Video satellite dish, Hartisheik camp, 1994

JENNY MATTHEWS/OXFAM

market in Hartisheik is now one of the most important in eastern Ethiopia, selling everything from Chinese thermos flasks to biscuits from the last food distribution. In the centre of the market, Beshir Yusuf runs the *Happy Video*. A large satellite dish sits on the roof of his corrugated iron building, and 40 or 50 people pay five Birr every night to watch cable TV. The wrestling is popular.

Returnees

Ethiopia's civil war created hundreds of thousands of refugees, who fled for safety to surrounding countries.

Many Ethiopia-born Somalis escaped to Somalia, fearing reprisals after the Ethiopian victory in the 1977/78 war with the Somali Republic. But the anarchy in southern Somalia after the fall of President Siad Barre drove them home again, creating another wave of human misery.

Awbare is a camp for such 'returnees'. Asked 'Where is home?', a woman in the camp warily and silently weighs the

answer. The wrong answer to the wrong person might end her entitlement to rations. Where would she like to be? *'Here.'* And if the rations stop? *'Wherever the rations are.'* In the long run, the international refugee industry may have bequeathed only one lasting thing to the Somali people: the word *ration* has entered the Somali vocabulary.

Resettlement

The refugees and returnees are not the only people to have been uprooted in Ethiopia. Thousands of others have been displaced during the last twenty years. Some moved because of drought or war; others were forcibly moved under the Mengistu government's two most ambitious programmes of social engineering: resettlement and villagisation.

About 600,000 people were moved to new areas under the massive resettlement programme of the 1980s. Resettlement was promoted as a long-term solution to population pressure and environmental degradation in the highlands. It seemed logical: people would be moved from overcrowded and unproductive areas into virgin lands elsewhere in the country, where they could start a new life.

But most of the people in the overcrowded regions of the north were unwilling to take the risk of settling in unknown regions of Ethiopia under any circumstances. The authorities ended up forcing people off to 'a better future' at gun-point. The supposedly 'virgin' lands to which they were transported were often occupied by local people of a different ethnic group, who resented the invasion. Some resettlers died on the road to their promised land, and thousands perished from disease and malnutrition after arrival. The land which seemed so green and promising to the planners lost its fertility after a few seasons, and couldn't sustain regular cultivation. One human rights organisation estimates that 50,000 people died during the operation.

Resettlement was in some ways a form of warfare. The head of the Workers' Party of Ethiopia for Tigray region,

Legesse Asfaw, was famous for repeating the saying: 'To kill the fish, you must drain the pond'. By forcibly removing people from rebellious regions in the north, the central government hoped, in vain, to terrorise the local populations into resisting the rebels.

Resettlement reached a peak in the mid-1980s, but the effects are still being felt. Thousands of unwilling resettlers have been unable to return home, and others, having made the return journey, are finding life harder than ever. Land, work, and housing are all in short supply.

'Villagisation'

In 1986, Qameru Ahmed, her husband and seven children were forced to move house. As part of a grandiose scheme typical of Mengistu's cruellest follies, she was to be uprooted so that, for the government, she would be easier to 'develop'.

Villagisation, which in some ways complemented the resettlement programme, was planned to bring Ethiopia's traditionally scattered homesteads into 'modern' villages, with rectangular houses arranged in straight lines.

In fact, Qameru was expected to move so that the government could more effectively tax and terrorise her family. When they came to her home area in eastern Harerghe region, all those who were reluctant to move were beaten or shot. The 'committee', composed of local people in the ruling party, had designated an area half an hour's walk away as the site of the new village. All the people who lived scattered among their fields, with enough space for some privacy and quiet, were now to be moved into a village in which the eaves of the houses overlapped. But the newhouses weren't even ready. If you didn't bribe the committee, they would burn your old house before you had taken all your possessions out.

People are normally on the move in much of Ethiopia: nomads in search of grazing, seasonal labourers following the harvests, or traders travelling to market.

Crossing a pass in an icy wind near Akesta in Wollo, six men are transporting big water pots on the backs of donkeys. The legs of one exhausted donkey buckle, and five jars strapped on its back topple and fall to the ground. One of the pots breaks. The men, some of them recently returned from resettlement areas, are taking them from Were Ilu, a nearby district blessed with good red pot-making earth, to sell in their villages just west of Dessie. A little petty trading is a lot of hard work. The profit on each jar will be about 50 pence. Three days' walk and sleeping rough for a total profit of £2.00. Ayalew Yimer takes his pots off the donkey's back and puts them on his head. 'Look at the life we lead,' murmurs one of his companions.

Ayalew, resettling again, this time back home in Wollo, is trying to augment his income from a tiny patch of land allocated to him by the local Peasants' Association. He came back with his wife and family to the area in 1991

after five years in a resettlement zone. He recalls the day in 1986 when officials came to his house and told him he had to move to Metekel, hundreds of kilometres to the west. When he refused, the party activists returned with soldiers and forced him and his family on to a bus. When they got to Metekel, he recalls, 'There wasn't much there, except malaria'. People could not move back to Wollo without the right travel documents, and so were effectively imprisoned.

But Ethiopia today has so many displaced, uprooted, and exiled populations that the upheavals are unlike anything previously experienced. From the destitute shanty-towns of Addis Ababa to the fly-blown returnee camps, there are many families who haven't been back to their place of origin for years, even decades, and are still waiting for the chance to feel once again the satisfaction of being back home.

Living off the land

Land is the backbone of Ethiopia's economy. In a country with almost no industry, land has been the only source of wealth for generations. There is hardly any aspect of national life which is not intimately related to questions of land ownership. It is one of the most critical political and economic issues for the future, and the most explosive of the past.

Until 1975, land in Ethiopia was organised on a feudal basis, with land-lords, including the Orthodox Church, owning almost all the land and letting it out to peasant farmers, who had to pay a large proportion of their harvest as rent. The complex web of family obligation, servitude, taxation, and feudal tribute payments developed into an intricate pattern of exploitation. In Wollo region, in 1974, it was estimated that over 100 different land-tenure systems were in place.

One of the most popular slogans of the Ethiopian Students' Movement, which provided some of the impetus for the revolution of 1974, was 'Land to the Tiller'. Only a year after the revolution, the Land Reform of 1975 nationalised all land, including that of the aristocracy and the church. This was perhaps the most popular thing the Derg ever did, and it has been retained in the new Ethiopian constitution of December 1994.

The problem is that cultivable land is scarce. Land holdings are small (on average, half a hectare per household in the highlands), and getting smaller, as the population increases and the soil is ever more degraded. One and a half million tonnes of soil are washed into the Blue Nile and other major rivers every year. In many areas the soil is only 35 cm deep. Rivers, loaded with topsoil, are the colour of milky instant coffee. More and more marginal land is coming under the plough in the overcrowded highlands, but experiments in exploiting virgin territory in the lowlands have had mixed results.

Scenes from the highlands

Dawn in Ajibar, a highland village in Wollo region, 2,700 metres high in the tropics, and it's cold. Cocks are crowing and the sun is only a promise behind banks of cloud in the east. The dew is heavy. Lammergeiers – menacing birds of prey – swoop overhead. Above them a jet passes on its way to Addis Ababa, 500 km to the south. A cow is being slaughtered on the edge of town, and a group of men stand around advising the butcher, and feeding on the liver. Raw meat is a delicacy in Ethiopia, and fresh liver is a special treat.

On a steep and rocky slope above a canyon, a man is ploughing in preparation for the short rains. There has been a little rain overnight and the ground is now soft enough to plough, in the hope of a crop of peas and beans. The ploughman shouts hoarsely to his two stumbling oxen, pulling a wooden plough tipped with iron. The cracks of his long whip echo across the gorge. Suspicious of outsiders, he'd rather not give his name. Other farmers walk by, carrying ploughs on their shoulders. The sun shines on the far side of the canyon. There has been revolutionary change in Ethiopia, but scenes such as these have changed little in hundreds of years.

Two young men walk by, with the determined long-distance gait of the Ethiopian on the road. They are returning home to Wollo, after a year working on a relative's farm far away in Jimma. They are on the fourth day of the walk from

Dessie, the regional capital. From his labours in Jimma, one of them has acquired a cassette radio: a meagre profit for a year's work, but he says his family will be pleased with the luxury, plus a little cash he has saved.

Wegedi, another town at the end of the road in Wollo, is linked to the rest of the region by a finger of rock bridging a mighty gorge. To the west is the great curve of the Blue Nile. Asked what they want to be when they grow up, children in Wegedi say manager, or driver, or doctor. Only one says he wants to be a farmer; he expects to get just half a hectare to plough, and half a hectare in the highlands is half a hectare of steep, rocky slope, which may have been farmed continuously for 5,000 years.

The rain, when it comes, is a massive force that takes away almost as much as it gives. The brown water foams over the landscape, scouring through gullies, taking the best soil with it. Hailstones batter crops in the fields. Settling on the hill-tops, the hail looks like a dusting of snow.

On the road

Trudging along the road are the *nagadis*: the traders moving coffee, sugar, and salt by donkey and mule train from the city to the villages. With a herd of about 20 pack animals, they make the trip once every two months during the dry season, when there is little work to do on the farm. Most of Ethiopia's produce is traded on four legs, not four wheels.

For truck drivers it is a bone-rattling, teeth-jarring ride up from northern Wollo to Makelle, the capital of Tigray. Hairpin bends in the mountain passes slow a food-aid convoy to walking pace. Hardly any of Ethiopia's 20,000 km of roads have any tarmac – and even they are full of pot-holes. It's a severe test of truck engineering and drivers' mettle. The threat of nocturnal bandit-raids breaks up the monotony of slogging up and down roads built by the Italian invaders in the 1930s.

The great Alamata plain opens up below: the scene of the first widely-broadcast TV footage of the 1984-85

Deforested and degraded slopes in the highlands: heavy rains wash thousands of tonnes of soil from agricultural land every year

famine. This is perhaps the only mental image of Ethiopia for many people in the outside world: the towering mountains in the background and the arena of death in the plain. Most of the year, the Alamata plain is green: thousands of hectares of sorghum and maize grow there. But only a few gnarled trees are dotted among the fields. Children climb up them and scare away the birds. A lone Oxfam water-tank stands sentinel by the roadside, the only sign of the largest feeding-camp during the famine period.

Scenes from the lowlands

The central highlands of Ethiopia – approximately the Abyssinia of old – contain most of the population, but are encircled and dwarfed in size by the lowlands, often the areas most recently added to the Ethiopian Empire. The edges of Ethiopia are hot, dry, neglected, and frequently unstable.

The landscape is dusty scrub, laced with dry river beds, and blessed with occasional springs and wells. A few towns on the main roads are separated by wide arid plains, dotted with herds of goats and camels.

Hauled into the Ethiopian state against their will during Menelik's reign, some people in the peripheral areas of Ethiopia have yet to accept the idea of belonging to the state called Ethiopia at all.

Herders or farmers?

Keeping animals, and following the best grazing, is the only way to live in the arid lands of lowland Ethiopia. Governments have tried to 'educate' the semi-nomadic peoples into settling down and farming, but it has been proved time and again that the nomads know how best to eke a living from an unforgiving environment, and that governments have ulterior motives. Nomads are difficult to tax or recruit for war, and they tend to take the law into their own hands when provoked. Placid sedentary peoples have always been the most useful for governments looking for soldiers, and raiders looking for slaves.

Cow's blood and milk are the staple food of any society in an arid area. It's a

The story of
Hadji Ahmed Adam

Hadji Adam, digging his land by hand to plant sorghum, used to be well-off: he has made his pilgrimage to Mecca. Now his land is reduced to one fifth of a hectare.

'I have this small piece of land here on this rocky hillside to provide food for my family. We've got another small plot in the valley for growing *qat*. I sell that in the market, and then we have a little money to buy extra food that we can't grow. My older children work as daily labourers. I have three sons and nine daughters. At home we have maize, sorghum, and wheat to eat, which my wife grinds. Maybe once every three or four months I can go to a Muslim hotel to eat meat. It's impossible to buy new clothes for the feast of Eid; we just have to wash our old ones.

'Once things were better. During Haile Selassie's time, I had a lot of land: enough to feed my family and live a good life. When the Derg replaced Haile Selassie, my land was redistributed among the members of the Peasant Association. I was left with a very small plot. I couldn't feed us. Now, after the Derg, there's no visible difference. The land is getting degraded, and the government isn't doing anything for poor farmers. The only difference is that now I can talk freely; but we don't have any more to eat.'

nutritious diet, and it can be sustained as
long as there is enough for the animals to
eat. In fact, if there is a drought, the cows
are too feeble to cope with the blood
letting, and they are left alone to feed as
best they can. To find enough for the
animals to graze on, boys and young men
go away from the homestead for months,
taking the animals hundreds of kilometres,
often across ethnic and political borders.

But the traditional diet has changed, as
other foods have become available. Roads
have penetrated into the remotest corners
of Ethiopia, and lowland people have
started trading animals for grain to vary
their diet, or selling animals for cash in
order to buy 'luxuries' like tea, sugar, and
clothes. In a drought, or during an
epidemic of cattle disease, the problems
mount up. Prices for animals drop,
because everyone is trying to sell before
their livestock wastes away. If there is a
drought throughout a whole region,
farmers who did manage to produce
something on their land will be able to
charge high prices for crops, and traders
from outside the area can make big
profits by trucking grain in.

Ethiopia has the largest population of
livestock in Africa, but it has dwindled
after a series of droughts all over the
country, and especially in the south-east.
While this gives the land a chance to
recover, it threatens the security of many
people. So more and more pastoralists are
growing maize, sorghum, and vegetables
in areas which were previously used only
for grazing. Popular myth would say that
nomads are too proud and set in their
ways to turn voluntarily to farming,
which they regard as a lowly occupation.
But there is a Somali proverb which says,
'When you fall down, it's only the land
that can support you.'

The wealth of the desert

Often described as a wilderness or a
desert, the lowlands produce livestock,
gums and resins, and hides and skins. A
certain type of black-headed sheep, raised
in the Ogaden and the Afar areas, is a
delicacy in the Gulf states. Livestock is

JENNY MATTHEWS/OXFAM

exported on the hoof through Somalia
and loaded on to ships for export.
Incense trees – gnarled dead-looking
bushes – are tapped to produce crystals
of sticky gum, also for export. Salt, mined
in the wilderness of the Ogaden and the
Danakil depression, is traded over
hundreds of kilometres. But perhaps the
most tantalising aspect of the lowlands'
wealth is natural gas in the Ogaden, and
oil in Gambella.

South-eastern Ethiopia lies on a
geological fault-line which also passes
through the oil-producing states of
Arabia. Prospectors – first Americans,
then Russians – have drilled in the region
for 20 years. Finally, sufficient deposits of
natural gas have been found to justify
commercial exploitation, and the World
Bank has invested about $150 million to
develop the Calub gas field. The more
romantic supporters of Ogadeni
independence look forward to their
region becoming the Kuwait of the Horn
of Africa. At the moment, however, there
is little to show except heaps of
machinery in the middle of nowhere.
None the less, it is one reason why
Ethiopian governments have clung on to
the Somali areas through thick and thin.

**Owning livestock is a
sign of wealth, but as
more and more land
comes under the
plough, grazing land
in the highlands is
increasingly scarce**

The environment: a broken covenant

Stone check-dams help to 'heal' a gully formed by the erosion that follows heavy rains. Top soil is trapped behind the dam, and over time the eroded land can be used for cultivation once more.

Forests once covered most of Ethiopia, and even in the 1950s there was six times more than there is now. Now only the west of the country is well wooded. Mighty broad-leaved trees spread a solid forest canopy as far as the horizon. Colobus monkeys and thousands of baboons and leopards live in the great western forests. Near the villages, coffee bushes are planted beneath the shade of other trees.

Elsewhere, tree felling, without replanting and without time for natural regeneration, has left Ethiopia's skin open to the elements. Only three per cent of Ethiopia's land is now forested. In schools and offices around the country, promotional posters present pictures of idealised villages, where every house has a little stand of eucalyptus trees and the elders gossip under a great fig tree.

The reality, however, in most of the country, is a scarred landscape, covered in open sores. When trees are cut down, the loose soil is washed away down to the bare rock, and bald patches pock the landscape.

At the market in Axum, Tigray, children squat in front of tiny piles of wood. One Birr (10 pence) buys about two kilos of roots and twigs. Wood is so scarce that armed soldiers at checkpoints on the roads search lorries and cars for it. Camel drivers from the lowlands, loaded with logs, travel at night to avoid the police and bring the wood to highland markets.

Eucalyptus is not the only tree

The eucalyptus, known in Ethiopia as the *bahir zaf*, 'the tree from overseas', was imported from Australia during the reign of Emperor Menelik. Ethiopian kings travelled on campaigns with huge retinues and, wherever they camped, they plundered the natural environment. By the time Menelik arrived in Addis Ababa, he had already abandoned one capital at Ankober, because the trees were all used up. The only reason why Addis Ababa survived to become today's metropolis was that the fast-growing eucalyptus was just about able to keep up with the city's voracious appetite for wood for fuel, construction, and cooking.

JENNY MATTHEWS/OXFAM

The eucalyptus has since become a distinctive part of the landscape. It's useful for many things. Private farmers grow it to sell poles for building. Some eucalyptus plantations at the Forestry Institute in Wondo Genet are even used for making perfume. But the price of fast growth is the eucalyptus' thirst for water. It copes with drought by sucking water away from a wide area around its trunk. Crops rarely grow well around a eucalyptus grove.

Tree nurseries are becoming a common sight, as development agencies and the government try to fix the soil and avert complete sterility. Seedlings are planted in rows of plastic cylinders, and are then distributed, usually free to all comers. The survival rate is regarded as good when half of them survive. As many as 40 million seedlings have been planted in Tigray in one year alone. Ethiopia's soil-conservation programmes are among the largest in the world. But it is a race against time, to save the soil and plant other varieties of tree seedling, especially indigenous species that (unlike eucalyptus) will provide forage for animals.

Akeza Tirumesh helping to build a stone terrace on a hillside in Tigray

Save our soils

On a bleak hillside in Tigray it's beginning to spit with rain. Wrapped against the morning cold in a cotton shawl as grey as the clouds above, Akeza Tirumesh humps rocks from one low dry-stone wall to another a few metres down the hillside. She and the other 15 men and women in her team have to pile up and repair three metres of terracing before they can go back home to a little warmth, and the reassurance that they will be eligible for food distributions from the Relief Society of Tigray (REST) next time round.

The ground is rocky and unyielding. Terracing is a series of miniature stone walls following the slope of the hill like the lines on a contour map. No crops grow there, so why are she and most of her village doing this seemingly futile job? 'To get food,' says Akeza, 'and help rebuild the country.' Akeza's three metres this Thursday form part of 200,000 km of terracing constructed in Tigray alone. The walls interrupt the flow of rainwater down the hill during the rainy season, stopping it from rushing torrentially into

Left: Bark is stripped off eucalyptus trees for use as fuel. The 5-year-old trees will be sold in the market.

Firewood on sale at Axum market

the rivers, and carrying with it heaps of valuable topsoil. Akeza's rations (a few kilos of wheat a week) are provided by REST in return for work. No work, no food. Any highlander can appreciate the Amharic proverb that says 'Only the locust can eat without working.'

It's not like the old days

Wherever you travel in Ethiopia, older people can always remember a time when things were not so hard, despite memories of war, famine, and oppression. Whether it's the price of eggs, or the quality of food, or the behaviour of the government, nostalgia is rife. In Tigray, up on the chilly hillside, women remember when they were young, and everything was plentiful: a time of butter, milk, and honey. Far away to the south in Wollayta, an Ethiopian nun, contemplating the latest drought, comments, 'The change of weather is confusing every farmer. Before, they could plan. Up to 1984 we always had rain in January.'

Something *has* happened in Ethiopia. A precarious environment has been devastated by desperate people. Poor farmers knew very well that they would have to pay the price for cutting down trees sooner or later. But the temptation to

sell charcoal to truck drivers along the roads when times were hard was too much to resist.

Unscientific it may be and not the whole story, but many people believe their present troubles are due to a change in the weather. An older Somali woman (80 years old by her own reckoning, counting years by rainy seasons) says that things were much better in her parents' time: you could support yourself with livestock rearing and farming. Now she is carrying a young baby on her back in the forlorn surroundings of Awbare (Teferi Ber) camp, where she arrived three years ago from a similar camp less than a day's walk away. She and many other people at Awbare have been refugees for at least ten years.

The covenant between humankind and nature has been broken throughout Ethiopia. When nature has failed to provide, humans have failed to preserve.

Farming and herding: the national lottery

Agriculture

Ethiopia lives off the land. Over three-quarters of the population depend on agriculture for their living, and over three-quarters of Ethiopia's export earnings come from agriculture and livestock. Most peasant farmers have to eke a living for their extended family from a plot of land not much larger than a suburban English garden. Only about 13 per cent of the land area can be used for crop production. The rest is forest, mountain, savannah, and pasture land.

Farming in Ethiopia is rather like playing roulette or the stock exchange. The rains, on which most people have to depend for their crops or livestock, often come too little or late – or sometimes too heavily. Only one per cent of land is irrigated. Farmers' only insurance is to hedge their bets by planting a variety of different crops that mature at different times, and to keep some seed in reserve to sow when the first attempts become dried up or waterlogged.

On the highlands and central plateaux, *teff*, barley, wheat, maize, beans, peas, and lentils are grown. At intermediate altitudes, farmers grow sorghum and millet. *Teff (eragrostis tef)* is the most valued food crop in Ethiopia, but you have to plough the land eight or nine times before planting it – and as many as one third of the subsistence farmers own no traction animals. In the southern highlands the 'false banana' tree (*enset*) is the main staple crop, with tubers, vegetables, and grains as secondary crops. Livestock husbandry, common as a subsidiary activity in all regions, is almost exclusively the only source of food production in the nomadic and semi-nomadic pastoralist lowland areas.

Farmers' survival strategies are highly sophisticated. The stakes are high: children are likely to sicken or die from malnutrition if parents make the wrong decision. They must balance high-yielding crops against drought-resistant types, and quick-maturing crops against slow-maturing crops. It is an art which is taught to the younger members of the family: boys go out ploughing with their fathers, girls look after the chickens, and all learn to watch the warning signs in nature from an early age.

Wooden paddles are used to winnow *teff*, Ethiopia's indigenous staple grain

JENNY MATTHEWS/OXFAM

A *jebena* is the traditional clay-fired coffee pot, used for the coffee ceremony

Stimulants to the economy: coffee ...

JENNY MATTHEWS/OXFAM

The pungent smells of frankincense and roasted coffee beans fill the room. A basket of popcorn or some *injera* (the national food, resembling a giant pancake) is passed around. The coffee ceremony is under way. Almost every day, a social ritual which transcends ethnic differences is played out all over Ethiopia. The family gathers and invites friends, relatives, or neighbours. All perch on stools while a woman – always a woman – heats water, sorts and roasts the green beans, and then pounds the roasted beans in a pestle and mortar. As they wait, people talk and work: spinning, basket weaving, and sewing often get done during the coffee ceremony.

Ethiopians claim that coffee originated in their country. (The Yemenis make the same claim.) There is a coffee-growing region called Kafa, which, according to the legend, gave coffee its name. About three-quarters of coffee grown in Ethiopia are consumed in the country. People brew up three times a day in the areas where it is grown.

'You have to work underneath it to get a good harvest,' says Gedi Turku, working in his plantation near Gazer in south-western Ethiopia. He has 100 or so trees, which produce a couple of sacks of coffee beans in a season. With 12 children and two wives to support, his cash crop is not making him rich. Most of the crop is sold on the local market: it's of indifferent quality.

The fragile coffee tree has had to support Ethiopia's foreign-exchange needs for decades. Coffee represents about two-thirds of the nation's export earnings. Ethiopia is the second-biggest producer of coffee in Africa, and the blends from Harar are regarded as among the best in the world. But a disease of the trees in the Hararghe region and unstable world prices have led many farmers to abandon coffee-growing, in favour of the stimulant *qat*.

Qat, chat, khat, miraa: it's all the same. The plant, catha edulis, looks like a privet hedge. Its leaves produce a stimulant around which much of the culture of eastern Ethiopia, Djibouti, Yemen, and Somalia revolves. First mentioned in the Ethiopian Royal Chronicles of the thirteenth century, it has a long lineage.

Consuming qat involves picking the young leaves and chewing them slowly in the corner of your mouth. Eventually the leaves disintegrate and the juices penetrate into the bloodstream. A mild amphetamine, it keeps you awake and rather jittery for hours, if you chew enough. Soft drinks, sugar, and sweet tea are offered during a qat session to help wash down the bitter taste.

Qat is grown in highland areas, where it is often the dominant cash crop. The market is lucrative, since much of the crop goes for export, to Djibouti and Somalia, generating valuable foreign exchange. In the highlands around Harar, qat grows in orderly rows for valley after valley.

Qat is popular with long-distance truck drivers and short-distance taxi drivers; a local joke says that it's not the qat which makes their driving erratic, it's the connoisseur's examination of every leaf which takes the driver's eyes off the road.

As with coffee, qat has its own ceremonies. In Somali areas, the men will gather in the heat of the afternoon on matting in the shade, and drink tea and chew over the burning issues of the day. Incense is burnt and cheap perfume is passed around to stimulate the senses.

Some qat addicts end up as desperate beggars in the cities. Because it suppresses the appetite, qat is chewed by people who do not have enough to eat. But the crop is a critical

... and qat

The leaves of qat are chewed for their stimulant properties

part of the export economy. The qat Exporters' Association fills up Ethiopian Airlines jets at Dire Dawa airport every day for export to Djibouti, and is a major economic force in the eastern region. The exchange rate between the Ethiopian Birr and the Somali shilling can fluctuate wildly when deliveries of qat arrive in a remote town.

Farmers have increasingly turned to qat as a relatively reliable, high-profit crop, which is often intercropped with vegetables like sweet potato. Prices for qat vary widely, according to the season. A good bunch can cost 80 Birr in the dry season, but only 10-20 in the wet season. Those who can irrigate their qat get rich. But when there is a drought, the qat growers suffer as much as the producers of other crops. 'Our bellies are like an empty road,' says one qat farmer. 'No one knows what happened to the rain – except God.'

Livestock

Ethiopia has the largest livestock population in Africa. About 40 per cent of agricultural production is made up of animal produce: meat, dairy products, and skins. Nearly every family, if they can afford it, will keep a few animals. Ownership and management of cattle and camels has often evolved into a form of social organisation in nomadic areas. Oxen for ploughing are a critical resource in the highlands. Sheep are kept in the mountains for wool and everywhere are reared for meat. Chickens and eggs are reared for market, or for eating as a delicacy at holiday times. Dairy products are an important part of children's diet, and tending smaller animals provides some women with their own small income.

Most of the camels in the world are in the Horn of Africa. About a million are in Ethiopia. Somalis and Afars alike keep camels for every purpose: as transport for their portable houses, for milk, for meat, and for insurance in times of war or drought. Camels are the glory of the Ogaden desert. Proverbs are written about them, blood feuds are settled by payment with them, and celebrations are enjoyed with their meat.

Owning oxen is one of the key distinctions between rich and poor in the highland farming areas. At least one third of farmers don't own even one ox. The ox is needed to pull the plough, which breaks up the soil, mixes up the moisture and the nutrients, and gives the tiny seeds of *teff* a chance. If you have one ox, you may be able to come to an arrangement with another farmer in the same position. If you have none, you borrow the ox for ploughing, but the owner will claim a portion – perhaps half – of your crop.

Goats, said Gandhi, are 'the poor man's cow'. Hardy but tasty, they are often tended by women and children in Ethiopia. There are about 15 different varieties in the country, and new breeds, mixed with the biggest and hardiest of the locals, are making a big contribution to some families' incomes. Abdurazak Mohammed, from the eastern Harerghe region, says 'It's like having something in hand, just in case you have an unexpected problem.' A goat can produce as much milk as a cow, if fed properly.

Traditionally, goats have been left to fend for themselves, but the state of the environment in Ethiopia is such that owners have to grow and collect greenery and forage for their animals: the land can't provide enough browse naturally.

As many as one third of farmers in Ethiopia own no traction animals for ploughing

MIKE GOLDWATER/OXFAM

Can Ethiopia feed itself?

When a guest is welcomed in an Ethiopian home, whether it is in the mountains or the desert, the custom is to offer everything possible, however poor the home. Coffee cups are filled to overflowing, and any less than three rounds would be considered rude. The generosity of Ethiopians is sometimes hard to believe. But more than half of the population are undernourished all the time.

Food unites Ethiopia like nothing else. There are few things that are found all over Ethiopia, but one of them is *injera*, the national food. Made from a variety of grains, with different sauces, the huge pancakes (as big as car tyres) are everywhere: red and crunchy *injera* made from sorghum in Humera on the north-west tip of Ethiopia; sticky grey and white versions made with maize in the Somali south-east; and everywhere the sour brown version made from *teff*, a tiny grain grown only in Ethiopia (and, in small quantities for homesick exiles, in North America). Rich in iron and high in gluten, *teff* is both the food on which the nation marches, and a key economic barometer. At one point during the war in Eritrea, the terms of barter were between sacks of *teff* and small Fiat cars, useless because of the lack of fuel. *Teff* is the most valued food crop in Ethiopia, and the agricultural cycle of its production is rooted deep in the country's culture.

Counting the calories

People eat little and not very often in Ethiopia. The average daily calorie intake is about 1,621 calories, about half that of North Americans (who eat on average 138 per cent of their actual requirements) and *less* than a standard relief ration is designed to provide. The daily per capita calorie supply is the lowest in Africa, just 71 per cent of requirements.

Meat is a rare luxury, and eating three times a day is the exception, not the rule. This is not a cultural matter, although fasting plays a major role in the lives of both Orthodox and Muslim Ethiopians. It is a matter of permanent hunger. Nearly

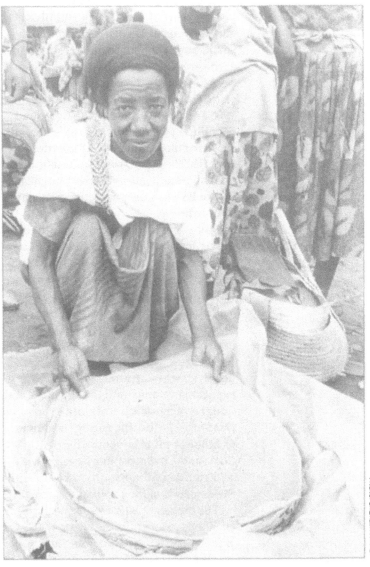

Take-away food: *injera* for sale at Jinka market

JENNY MATTHEWS/OXFAM

39

two-thirds of those children who manage to survive their first five years are physically stunted, and their mental development is inhibited by malnourishment.

The food 'emergencies' that frequently swallow up large amounts of food aid in Ethiopia occur with regularity because the normal state of the nation's belly is half-empty. It doesn't take much to tip the balance from underfeeding to famine. Easily-treated problems caused by vitamin deficiencies, such as goitre and night blindness, are also common.

More mouths to feed

Ethiopia can nearly feed itself: it even produced 80 per cent of its food in the famine years of 1984-85. Statistically, the gap between needs and production is small, but in human terms it is a margin of misery and death. Closing the gap is possible, if only the population remains static. But it has already quadrupled since 1900 and, with a current total of around 54 million people, Ethiopia is the second-most populous nation in Africa after Nigeria. The remorseless arithmetic of an annual growth rate of 2.9 per cent means that in 25 years the population may have doubled.

More than half of all Ethiopians are under sixteen. On average, 7,000 children are born in Ethiopia every day, of whom one in five will die before his or her fifth birthday. Life-expectancy at birth is only 46 years, while family planning is used by only two per cent of couples, mainly in urban areas.

Progress has been made since 1960, however, when an Ethiopian could expect to live only until the age of 36, and under-five mortality was close to one third of all births. The natural resources of Ethiopia could support a larger population, but economic development will have to be dramatic to catch up with the demands of the population.

The problem that stares farmers and economic planners in the face is that weather patterns are becoming increasingly unpredictable, and pressure on the land from over-grazing and incessant cultivation has reduced soil fertility in many areas. Per capita food production has been declining by about two per cent a year. If this trend continues, people will go hungrier and hungrier; or food imports will have to grow by about ten per cent every year, just to keep the Ethiopians at their present inadequate level of nutrition.

Even the most optimistic forecasts for Ethiopia's food production predict a perennial shortfall of at least half a million tons every year for the next twenty years. In today's money, importing that amount of food and delivering it where it is needed costs about $200 million each year: more than Ethiopia ever earned from coffee exports.

Food aid

There is a joke circulating in Ethiopia, probably coined by a cynical aid worker: 'When there's a drought, we pray for rain in Canada.' Canada, the USA, and the European Union have provided huge quantities of food aid over the last decade. Since 1985, well over half a million tons of food have been delivered to Ethiopia every year. In the next five years, imports will probably need to rise to one million tons a year to keep Ethiopia on an even keel.

But imported wheat, which makes up most of Ethiopia's food aid, is not to local people's taste. Most highlanders would prefer *teff*, the staple grain which grows in only very small quantities outside Ethiopia; lowlanders are more accustomed to maize. Locally-made butter (*kibe*) is part of the distinctive flavour of Ethiopian *wat* sauces, and imported edible oil is no substitute.

The paraphernalia of food aid has developed into a market all of its own: the tin cans, plastic jerry cans, barrels, and sacks of imported food are now ubiquitous all over the country. When the US military donated millions of army rations left over from the Gulf War, the brown plastic wrapping was made into hats, bags, school satchels, and shoes.

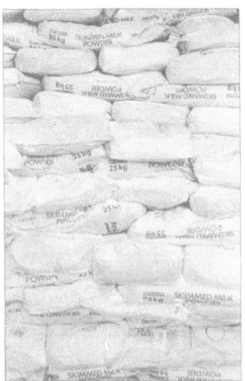

Drought-cracked soil and food-aid packages: reminders of Ethiopia's vulnerability to food shortages

Donated oil containers make tea kettles, and USAID bags, emblazoned 'Not to Be Sold or Exchanged', are furiously traded in Dire Dawa to carry locally produced food.

Food aid is calculated in a methodical way. Its scientists are nutritionists, agronomists, and logisticians. In order to determine Ethiopia's food-aid needs, a notional number of kilos is decided as the average annual consumption per head. This, multiplied by the number of needy people, becomes the food requirement. Then the harvest is estimated, and the difference becomes the basis of an appeal to international donors. In famines, children are weighed and their height measured against global standards devised in the USA decades ago. If over 20 per cent of children fall below 80 per cent of normal, a 'nutritional emergency' can be declared.

But this systematic calculation of need is followed by a haphazard system of distribution. Any of about 100 voluntary agencies may undertake to distribute food; when deliveries falter, rations often differ widely from place to place. Some food is given in return for work, some is not; some is given as a balanced food basket – grains, oil, and pulses – but elsewhere people receive just grains. None of this indicates mismanagement: feeding millions of people in Ethiopian circumstances is a logistical nightmare; but it does make it almost impossible to trace the impact of food aid.

There is no doubt that Ethiopia needs help with food. And the European Union and North America usually have stocks to spare. Very roughly, it costs less than £10.00 a month to save an Ethiopian from starvation. The real debate is not about the *cost* of food aid, but about whether it will be a permanent feature of the Ethiopian economy. It is hard to imagine that there will be enough money and goodwill among the donor countries to develop long-term solutions that really work, and gradually enable a few more people to become self-sufficient in food every year – when just keeping the country on its knees is costing billions.

The world's second-poorest economy

Too poor to buy money

Ethiopia can't afford new banknotes as often as richer countries, and every note is passed around until it has the consistency of tissue paper encrusted with grease. Sometimes stapled together, damaged notes are hard to get rid of in areas far from a bank, and forgeries are not uncommon. The currency, the

Gebremeskal Gebre Aregawi earns his living making sandals from used car tyres

Ethiopian Birr, is in tatters, both physically and economically.

Ethiopia has embarked on a Structural Adjustment Programme which is meant to stimulate economic growth and benefit the agricultural sector. Relaxation of the rigid economic policies of the Derg era has encouraged farmers to plant more, and traders' business is expanding. But despite superficial signs of economic life, urban unemployment is rampant, and the ranks of the poor grow larger all the time.

Ethiopia was often called 'the poorest country in the world', ranking last in the World Bank's statistics of gross national product (GNP) per head. The miserable honour now belongs to Mozambique, and Ethiopia is 'only' the second-poorest nation. Switzerland is the richest country in the world by this indicator, with an annual GNP per capita of $33,610, compared with Ethiopia's $120. UNICEF estimates that about 62 per cent of the population live below the absolute poverty level, which means they are unable to afford an adequate diet and other basic necessities.

An economy addicted to coffee

Agriculture is the foundation of the Ethiopian economy. To pay for imports of petroleum and machinery, the country exports hides and skins, oil-seeds, and pulses. But coffee is the main export item, generating 60 per cent of Ethiopia's foreign-exchange earnings. This is a dangerous dependency: when coffee prices drop on international markets, Ethiopia loses millions of dollars in revenue. The coffee-producing countries used to be organised into a cartel, to try to maintain higher prices by holding back

excess produce from the market. But
when competitive pressure forced the
agreement to collapse in 1989, the
resulting free-for-all meant that
consumers in rich countries enjoyed the
cheapest coffee in years. Coffee prices hit
rock bottom in 1993; in 1994 they shot up
after the Brazilian harvest failed – only to
fall again by the end of the year. At best,
coffee-production offers only a precarious
living. If a health scare in the USA and
Europe were to lead to a drop in coffee
consumption, the Ethiopian economy
would be ruined.

Ethiopia's trade deficit, US$822 million
in 1992 on a balance-of-payments basis,
reflects the fact that international terms of
trade have successively moved against
the country since 1970. Ethiopia must
find alternatives to the export of
agricultural products on which it has
always relied. The exploitation of mineral
resources offers some hope of eventually
reducing the nation's trade deficit. In the
south-west, at Kenticha, a significant
deposit of tantalite, a mineral used in the
electrical components industry, has been
identified for mining. Exploration is in
progress to locate natural gas and oil
fields in the Ogaden, and an oil concess-
ion has been granted in the Afar region.

Ethiopians have been getting poorer
for the last 25 years. Growth in gross
domestic product has averaged 1.5 per
cent each year: not enough to keep up
with the high rates of population growth.
The civil war consumed up to half of the
government's budget at its height. The
black-market exchange rate rose until it
was three times the official rate, and
public-service wages were frozen. Out of
its meagre resources, Ethiopia paid
nearly $100 million in interest alone on
debt in the financial year 1991/92.
Arrears have accumulated, because debt-
servicing obligations were not met. In
1991 the Transitional Government
inherited an economy on its knees. The
next year, the total external debt was 66
per cent of the country's gross national
product, and the debt-service ratio was
14 per cent of export earnings.

Although the bulk of Ethiopia's long-
term debt is owed to bilateral creditors,
half of this is owed to former Eastern Bloc
allies of the Mengistu regime. The largest
single creditor is the former USSR.
Repayment of the rouble debt accrued for
the purchase of arms during the civil war
is repugnant to Ethiopians.

Cancellations of external debt are
critical for the recovery of Ethiopia's

JENNY MATTHEWS/OXFAM

Trading home-grown cotton in Axum. Ethiopia's internal market has begun to expand since the end of the civil war, but the country needs to earn foreign exchange with a strong and sustainable export trade.

economy, so that the foundations can be laid for its sustained growth. Ethiopia's bilateral creditors in the Paris Club agreed to cancel half their debt at the end of 1992, with the balance rescheduled over 25 years. But it is the multilateral creditors, principally the World Bank, which have the power to make the most significant concessions on debt-relief. Their goodwill depends on Ethiopia's commitment to economic reform and a structural adjustment programme.

Economic reform

A Policy Framework Paper, devised by the government with the IMF and World Bank, presented an economic plan up to 1994/95. This policy was well received by donors, and has produced pledges of over $1 billion of new aid money. The reform programme foresees growth of 5.5 per cent over the next few years. `

The economic reforms will hit some people hard. Redundancies in the public sector and privatised industries, and anticipated inflation due to lack of control over producer prices, will increase urban poverty. Some of the options to catch these poor people in a safety net include public-sector wage rises (the first was simultaneous with the devaluation of the Birr in October 1992); severance pay and retraining for sacked government workers; and food and kerosene vouchers and labour-based public works to help the urban poor.

As such, Ethiopia's Structural Adjustment Programme is fairly typical of the kind of policy which the World Bank and IMF have recommended for many poor countries. It has begun without dramatic increases in costs for public services like education and health, which are often the bitterest pill to swallow. But neither has it produced anything tangible to help the poor, other than the faint hope of a 'trickle-down' effect. There is a long way for a very little money to trickle down in Ethiopia, and a special poverty-alleviation package was discussed at great length at the start of the economic reforms, in order to tackle the problem more directly. So far, nothing has been decided. Ethiopians may have to wait a long time before they see any benefits from the Structural Adjustment Programme.

Education: a way out of poverty?

A school with no desks

At the Obelisk School in Axum, 854 students attend in two shifts, morning and afternoon. Many children, from the age of 6 upwards, come from 10 km away. The school is not unusual by Ethiopian standards: it has no desks, no chairs, and not even a football. There is no water tap and no toilet. Perched on little heaps of stones for four hours under a canopy of dried branches, the children are learning mathematics. Visitors are greeted with a loud 'Good morning, Teacher' and a few giggles. The school director, Tekle Gebre Egziabher, sits in a small room, floored with red earth, and roofed with corrugated iron. 'We have no budget,' he explains, 'to buy a football or volleyball.' Two posts in the dusty field behind the tiny buildings might once have had a net strung between them, a long time ago. The only source of cash for the school is the fee of 50 pence a year paid by each student. The central government pays the teachers' salaries, but everything else has to come from the parents – who have little to spare.

Nationally, only about 22 per cent of children are enrolled in primary school, and only about 10 per cent make it to secondary school. These rates are among the lowest in Africa. The UN Development Programme estimates that the average member of the workforce in Ethiopia has only one year of schooling. Despite major campaigns during the Mengistu years, only about half of Ethiopians can read and write.

Many schools work on a shift system, opening three times a day to handle the overwhelming number of students. Classes of 100 pupils are not uncommon. When high schools break for lunch in Addis Ababa, traffic grinds to a halt, and hundreds of children spill on to the streets.

An elementary school in Tigray: no desks, chairs, water, or toilets. 843 pupils walk up to 10 km to get there.

An alphabet with 256 letters

Progress in education in Ethiopia is not simply a question of increased enrolments. The curriculum has been radically revised. In the past, all schools in Ethiopia taught and tested in Amharic. (The universities used English.) Children who spoke other languages had to learn Amharic before being able to understand anything at school. It was a major hurdle to overcome: learning a foreign language, with its 256-letter alphabet and ferociously difficult grammar, made academic progress hard. As part of the regional decentralisation policy, new curricula and school books have been drawn up, and children can now be educated in their mother tongue in over a dozen Ethiopian languages. Most of the languages are written with the Latin alphabet.

So many adults have had their education disrupted by the war that it is common to see grown-ups sitting at the back of the class in primary schools. The fighters of the EPRDF are also catching up with their education, and groups of them walk back from classes, satchel in one hand, Kalashnikov in the other.

Literacy class for workers at Hayhaile tree nursery, Tigray

If Ethiopia is to diversify its economy, and be less dependent on agriculture, it will need a skilled work force to develop light industry, tourism, and other revenue-generating economic sectors. A well-educated generation of young people who can find worthwhile work may be the best insurance against drought for Ethiopia. Girls and boys at present are unlikely to complete even primary school, which leaves them only limited 'career' options. More children in school, especially more girls, will help to widen the scope of the potentially employable.

አካባቢያችን እንክብካቤ ዶፈልጋል። የተፈጥሮ ሀብታችንን በዐቅድ መጠቀም አለብን። የሚተካ ሀብትን ከሥር ከሥሩ ለመተካት የሚያስችል ሰልት መቀየስ ያስፈልጋል። የሜሬት አጠቃቀም ማጠቅ ያስፈልጋል። የመናፍርያ፣ የመዝናኛ፣ የእርሻ፣ የደን ወዘተ. ብሎ መከፋፈል ይገባል። እንደ አካባቢው ሁኔታ ለሚታረሰው መሬት እርከን መሥራት ያስፈልጋል።

የምናረባቸውን ከብቶች ብዛት መወሰን ጠቃሚ ነው። ለከብቶች በቂ ግጦሽ እንዲኖራቸው ያስፈልጋል። በዘፈቀደ ከብት ማርባት አካባቢን ችግር ላይ ይጥላል።

ደንን መንከባከብ አለብን። አንድ ዛፍ ስንቆርጥ በምትኩ ሌላ መትከል ይኖርብናል። የቤተሰባችንን ብዛት ከአቅማችን ጋር ማመዛዘን አለብን።

አካባቢያችን እንዳይበክል ጥንቃቄ ማድረግ አለብን። ቆሻሻ የትም እንዳይጣል ያስፈልጋል።

Women's lives: the 15-hour day

Despite all the rhetoric during the Mengistu era about the noble role of women in 'socialist Ethiopia', women continue to be ignored, exploited, and undervalued. About 14 per cent of rural households in Ethiopia are headed by women, and the figure rises to 22 per cent in urban areas. Like most women all over the world, rural women work at home without pay. Collecting fuel-wood and water, raising children, and working in the fields and with livestock all add up to a staggering burden. A woman's average working day is 15 hours long. Men produce about the same amount as women, but men have far fewer tasks in the running of the household. In paid employment, women are under-represented: fewer than one quarter of government workers are women.

Only one in four girls ever goes to school at all. Girls drop out of school because they are needed at home to work. And they marry young: ten per cent of girls between 10 and 14 are married. Women have less access to land, labour, capital, information, credit, and government assistance than men. Their subordination to men in terms of money and property was even included in the Civil Code of 1960. Women did not win the right to vote until 1956.

Marriage and motherhood

Each Ethiopian woman bears, on average, five children, but nearly ten per cent of women give birth to ten live babies in their lifetimes. At least 10,000 women die in child-birth every year. Almost every child is born at home, in unhygienic conditions, with a local untrained midwife in attendance. Some traditional practices, like coating the umbilical cord with cow dung or leaving the baby unattended until the placenta is delivered, cause extra problems. And when things go wrong, the traditional midwife can only do so much. Goats are slaughtered, massage is performed, but often it is too late. Women sometimes arrive in a hospital or clinic after 48 hours of exhausting labour.

Some estimates suggest that as many as 90 per cent of Ethiopian women are

Kahsa Girmay carrying her baby in a goatskin pouch

JENNY MATTHEWS/OXFAM

circumcised. Frequently described as 'female genital mutilation', the removal of parts of the outer sex organs is a cultural practice common throughout the Horn of Africa. The risk of infection from unsterilised razor blades or knives, and the risk of excessive bleeding, are high. The operation is often performed on girls when they are as old as ten, and medical and social problems develop later in life. Sexual intercourse can be painful and childbirth dangerous. Infections are common.

In many countries it has been shown that women with more education have fewer children, because they appreciate that spacing children is better for the health of the mother, and gives a child a greater chance of surviving past the age of five. Without education, an ideal family size might be 'whatever God gives us'. Most women have little control over how many children they have, and modern contraception services are simply not available. Some recent studies indicate that nearly half of Ethiopian couples would like to be able to plan their families, but are unable to. Condoms are being distributed as part of the AIDS-control programme in their hundreds of thousands, but few people outside the cities use them.

New challenges for women

It would be foolish to expect traditions which dictate women's lives to be broken in the space of a generation or two, whatever the government's stated development priorities. Domestic violence and rape are rarely even discussed in public. However, some of the dislocations in the recent history of the Horn of Africa have produced opportunities for women as an unexpected benefit. Some refugee women, for example, have found more responsibility and respect in camp life than in their previous nomadic existence. But many others have fallen prey to rapists in the same camps. Women were fighters and even tank-commanders in the civil war, but find themselves unemployed in peace time. Many have been widowed. But the break-up of families by war and poverty has created more women-headed households with some degree of recognition in the community.

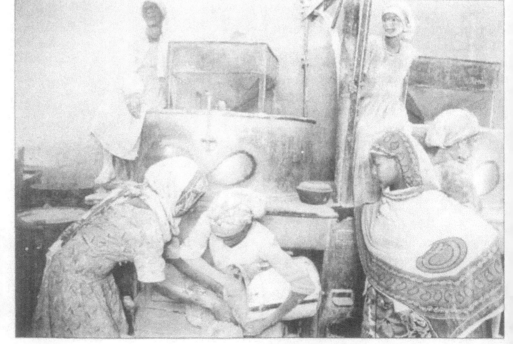

Grinding mill at Adwa. Women value their local community mill, because grinding grain by traditional methods at home is their heaviest task.

'May God grant you health'

Walking through groves of banana, coffee, avocado, and papaya, women carry huge bunches of bananas to market. In the other direction, stretchers made of sticks and woven banana leaves bring the sick to the clinic at the end of the road. A mother-and-child health session is held at the clinic once a month. Mothers assemble under the shade of a tree deep in the Wollayta hills and are given some health-education talks while they wait their turn. Christian and traditional prayers are offered. Some fathers come carrying children too. Children are weighed in a red washing-up bowl hanging from a tree.

The most common greeting in Amharic, Ethiopia's lingua franca, is *Tenasystillin*; loosely translated, it means 'May God grant you health'. The greeting, far too often, is in vain. Ethiopians die young: one fifth of all children die before their fifth birthday, and the average life expectancy is 29 years less than in the UK.

Teshona Tona has been brought by his older brother to the clinic in Wollayta. Aged four, he weighs only seven kilos, and is just starting to walk. Every child attending a clinic like this one is given a yellow health card. It records the name and date of birth (when known), vaccinations, and weight. The weight graph covers the first five years of the child's life, and shows a gently rising curve of normal weights for the age. Teshona has never been charted in the 'normal' area of the graph. His growth chart is a nearly horizontal line.

Diseases on the point of extinction in many other countries – tuberculosis, polio, and leprosy, for example – are still rampant in the Ethiopian countryside. But the greatest killer is diarrhoea.

Four-year-old Teshona Tona, badly malnourished, is carried by his brother to a clinic in Wollayta. Teshona's yellow card records details of his history and treatment.

Infections prey on malnourishment, and disease makes eating almost impossible. This is the vicious cycle of disease and malnutrition. The ravages of a simple, preventable disease are appalling: half a million children die under the age of five *every year*. This is only slightly less than the number of people who died in the famine of 1984-1985. In the UK, with a similar population, the annual figure for under-five mortality is 7,000.

At the clinic in the Wollayta hills, hard-pressed health workers see a stream of patients all morning. The most common diseases are malnutrition, malaria, tuberculosis, and infections of the chest or eyes. Sister Martha keeps a little square of paper on her desk and puts a mark against the types of illness which people are presenting. 'One died', she writes: another small statistic in Ethiopia's health records.

49

Hiwot, meaning *Life*, is the name of the brand of condom being sold in Ethiopia as part of an AIDS-prevention campaign

AIDS

HIV infection and AIDS have yet to take hold in Ethiopia on the scale seen in many African countries. Thanks to political, geographical, and economic isolation, Ethiopia has been to some extent insulated from the pandemic. While other countries count cases of HIV infection in millions, and AIDS deaths in hundreds of thousands, by November 1994 the Ministry of Health in Ethiopia had recorded only 15,565 cases of full-blown AIDS since 1986. There is, however, no reason for complacency. Official statistics are, as usual, likely to show only the tip of the iceberg. Ethiopia is opening up politically, and the slow-burn nature of the disease means that, in some cases emerging now, patients were infected before any public education began in the mid-1980s. The steep upward curve of AIDS cases is reflecting, in miniature, the rampage of the disease in other countries.

Addis Ababa is by far the worst-affected place, but the disease is spreading into the remotest countryside, helped in particular by the demobilisation of the Mengistu army. There could be few more effective ways of spreading the disease than sending half a million soldiers back from garrison towns to their villages. Transmission by heterosexual intercourse is the most common route of infection now, but some traditional practices are likely to increase the incidence of the disease. Circumcision, tattooing, and decorative scarification are all common in Ethiopia. Unless performed with sterile blades, they pose an additional risk. Ethiopia's AIDS Control Programme has launched a 'Life' brand condom which is selling in the cities, but it would be naive to suggest that it is widely available or popular in the rural areas.

Surviving in the city

Mercedes cars and donkeys vie for space on Addis Ababa's potholed streets. What began as a temporary encampment of Emperor Menelik and his retinue, on the site of Oromo hot springs, has turned into a metropolis of four million people. Still the diplomatic centre of Africa, hosting the Organisation of African Unity and the UN's Economic Commission for Africa, Addis Ababa is also the meeting point for all of Ethiopia's many peoples.

Barefoot shepherds lope along past prostitutes in black leather mini-skirts; beggars implore ambassadors for change; Nuers from the West talk pidgin Amharic with Somalis from the East; Orthodox mystics and foreign evangelists stir up their respective congregations. Not quite harmonious enough to be called a melting pot, Addis Ababa is a series of villages, loosely interconnected but often ethnically defined.

More and more people are leaving the countryside to seek their fortune in Addis Ababa. And the more people who arrive, the less the city's facilities can cope. Ethiopia has had one of the lowest rates of urbanisation in Africa, but Addis Ababa and other centres like Dessie, Dire Dawa, and Makelle have grown dramatically since the end of the civil war. Soldiers have returned home, travel and residence regulations have been

Addis Ababa is the meeting point of old and new, town and country. Here, goats drowse outside a garage.

relaxed, and petty business is flourishing. Sadly, the city's streets are often not paved at all, let alone paved with gold. As less than half the population have a latrine, the streets are often open sewers.

Poverty and squalor are rife. Children collect pine needles from trees overhanging the presidential palace to use for cooking fires; a group of homeless people sleep under plastic sheeting just below Mengistu's Stalinist monument to the revolution; and children compete with birds of prey and dogs to scavenge among the bins outside expatriate apartment blocks. Many people rarely touch cash, surviving on a system of barter and work, in return for room and board. The minimum wage of 100 Birr in the cities is a legal fiction: some domestic servants earn less than £5.00 a month. This is not far from slavery.

In cities and villages, a form of social security is provided by traditional institutions such as mutual savings groups, called *ekub*, which take a monthly contribution from members and then pay out when someone is in trouble or needs a lump sum for a wedding, for example.

Savings associations for funerals are generally called *eddir*. These networks are dominated by women. It has been estimated that tens of millions of Birr pass through the *ekubs* every month in Addis Ababa.

Local churches and mosques do more to save the poor from beggary or prostitution – the two last-ditch options for Ethiopian men and women – than any other organisation. Missions and church groups run soup kitchens, health and sanitation programmes, small savings and credit schemes, and construction programmes to provide some sort of safety net for poor neighbourhoods in the cities. The best programmes may lend a few hundred Birr to a family to pay for the equipment needed to make beer or take-away food; the loan is repaid in a series of small instalments, then recycled as a loan to another mini-entrepreneur.

The streets of Addis Ababa are not paved with gold. An old man survives by sleeping rough and scavenging.

A land of righteousness

Religious belief plays a central part in the day-to-day life of Ethiopians. Whether in the home or in a place or worship, God, Allah, or traditional deities are supplicated, thanked, and held responsible for the ups and downs of life. Religion has played a key role in history, and today is one of the dividing lines of society and politics.

The most remarkable feature of Ethiopia's religious life is the centuries-old coexistence of three of the world's main religions. In and around Gonder, Ethiopian Jews, Christians, and Muslims lived together in peace until very recently.

The Falasha

Ethiopia's links with the pre-Christian Holy Land are confirmed by the survival of a 'lost tribe' of Jews, who lived in northern Ethiopia around the city of Gonder. Known by Ethiopians as *Falasha* ('strangers') and to themselves as the *Bete Israel* ('house of Israel'), they lived according to a mixture of Jewish and Ethiopian traditions.

Numbering about 40,000 in the early 1980s, the Falasha were recognised as Jewish by the Israeli rabbinical authorities, although they conducted their ceremonies in *Ge'ez*, the ancient Ethiopic language. As war and famine ravaged their region, the Falashas looked for a way out. According to the Israeli law of return, they had the right to Israeli citizenship. Israel, in a shadowy deal with dictator Mengistu Haile Mariam, arranged the evacuation of the Falasha in two dramatic airlifts: one from Sudan in 1985, and the other, known as 'Operation Solomon', in the last days of the Ethiopian civil war in May 1991. But the Falashas' deliverance has been mixed.

Arriving in Israel at the same time as hundreds of thousands of Russian immigrants, most of the Ethiopian Jews have failed to find work or permanent housing. Their clerical autonomy was threatened when Israeli authorities refused to recognise their spiritual leaders, or *kessim*. A unique part of Ethiopia's cultural heritage has been lost, and the Falashas' dreams of the promised land have been disappointed.

The Orthodox Church

The Christian heritage of Ethiopia pre-dates that of Europe. When Europeans were still pagan, the Christian faith was taking root in Ethiopia. Ethiopian Orthodoxy was founded in 341 AD, after two Christian Syrian boys, shipwrecked off the Red Sea coast, were brought to the court of the Emperor of Axum. Eventually they succeeded in converting his successor, Emperor Ezana, to Christianity. From there the religion spread far and wide, encouraged by early missionaries from Syria.

Orthodox Christianity is divided into the Russian, Greek, Syrian, and Ethiopian Orthodox churches. They differ from the rest of Christianity in their use of the old Julian religious calendar, the composition of their scriptures (there are 81 books in the Orthodox Bible, against 57 in the King James version), and their rituals.

The Ethiopian Orthodox Church has incorporated elements of Judaism and even, possibly, ancient Egyptian religious ceremonies into its Christian faith. Its practices are arcane, complex, and almost unfathomable to the uninitiated. It is a severe and ascetic faith. Judaic laws on diet and circumcision are followed strictly. A priest in Lalibela may spend about 12 hours a day at the church, with

A priest displays priceless processional crosses at the Church of the True Cross, Lalibela

Sunday ceremonies starting at midnight. The devout pray seven times a day, and fast on 180 days in the year. Hermits live in the woods and caves around the monasteries. During times of persecution, churches were built in the most inaccessible places, on cliff-tops, islands, and mountains. But at the height of its power, the church amassed huge wealth: it owned fifteen per cent of the land, and collected rent and tax from its tenants. Even today, the Church wields a major influence on national politics and local lives.

It is estimated that there are 20 million Christians in Ethiopia. The Church itself claims 38 million. Today the clergy number about 200,000, scattered in 15,000 churches. A Sunday communion ceremony (*Qidasse*) needs two priests and three deacons to officiate. Much of the church liturgy is conducted in *Ge'ez*, the parent language of the Ethiopian highlands – the Latin of Ethiopia. Even when the sermon and other parts of the ceremony are conducted in Amharic, the nation's modern *lingua franca*, much of the ritual is incomprehensible to the Ethiopian listener.

The Church today is still strong, despite the confiscation of its property, the politicisation of its leadership, and the uncomfortable encounter with Marxist atheism during the Mengistu regime. Even those who do not attend church observe some of the customs of the faith, bowing three times towards a church, even when passing in a taxi in Addis Ababa, and stopping priests in the street to kiss their hands.

Islam in Ethiopia

Ethiopia's first refugees were Muslims. While the prophet Mohammed was still alive, some of his disciples took refuge in Ethiopia from persecution in Arabia. As a result, the Prophet dubbed Ethiopia 'a land of righteousness where Allah will give you relief from your suffering'. The faith has grown in Ethiopia ever since, in periods of violent conflict with Christians, interspersed with centuries of peaceful cohabitation.

Muslims probably number as many as Christians in today's Ethiopia; the precise count is a highly contentious issue. Given Ethiopia's historical reputation as a

Right: One of 87 mosques in Harar. The town is one of the most important Islamic centres in the world.

54

Christian redoubt, it has not been easy for Muslims to assert themselves in the modern state. None the less, Ethiopia has a rich Islamic history. Harar is to Ethiopian Islam as Axum is to the Orthodox Church. The oldest mosque in the Horn of Africa stands at the centre of the walled city of Harar, founded in 1520. The Juma'a mosque, founded by Sheik Abadir, proved to be a magnet for the surrounding villages, and five of the main settlements moved into the town. The Sheik is buried at a shrine beneath the huge branches of an old fig tree in a corner of the old city.

Harar grew into a powerful trading centre, exporting slaves, ivory, coffee, tobacco, cloth, livestock, honey, spices, and incense. By now the city has accumulated a total of 87 mosques and 103 shrines and is one of the most important Islamic centres in the world. A dusty museum holds manuscript copies of the Koran, 800 years old, bound in leather and exquisitely inscribed on goatskin.

Ethiopia's Muslims are Sunni, the largest branch of Islam. As with the Orthodox Christians, traditional beliefs in natural spirits have been amalgamated into the monotheistic religion of Islam. The relationship between the two is best described by an Oromo proverb: 'His mouth talks about Sheik Hussein [a place of pilgrimage], but his hands are stretched up to the tree.'

The old religion

Older than all the monotheistic religions with their written scriptures are the animist beliefs of Ethiopia's 80 ethnic minority groups. At least a quarter of these groups are less than 20,000 strong. They are generally on the edges of the country, mainly in the lowlands, speaking an array of unique languages, and leading their lives according to the seasons.

The Hamer people, probably about 15,000 in number, live in the far south-west of Ethiopia. They are a traditional pastoralist society, rearing animals for blood, milk, and sometimes meat, and growing sorghum in a few rain-fed areas. The idea of nation states and lines on the map mean little to them. What is important is their Hamer territory, enclosed by a range of mountains to the east, beyond which live the Tsemhai people, and the Omo river, controlled by the Geleb group to the west.

Much photographed for coffee-table books, but rarely interviewed, traditional peoples know their land better than any government official or outsider. Eking a living from the arid expanses of Ethiopia's periphery is a skill, but young civil servants in the government ministries still talk of the 'backwardness' of the 'nomads', and argue that settlement is the way forward for them.

The traditional peoples of Ethiopia are woven together by systems of age groups, marital alliances, clan allegiance, and water rights. But their way of life is under pressure: the easy availability of guns, the shortage of land and water, and the threat of AIDS have all made life on the periphery even more precarious. All of Ethiopia's minority peoples are facing change. Pressure on land and livestock has meant that many, like the Hamer, are having to cultivate and become semi-sedentary. Most of their languages have never been written down.

Surha Ado, an elder of the Arbore people, says that life has become more difficult. 'All we know is how to follow

Shiferew Ibeda, a Hamer man, with his gun. Weapons of war are everywhere in Ethiopia.

the seasons,' he says. 'If there was a drought, we used to hunt.' But the seasons are not reliable any more, and the wild-life is fast disappearing. His people now depend on rations from the government Relief and Rehabilitation Commission. 'It was never like this before,' he says, echoing a theme voiced by older people all over Ethiopia. 'You don't even get milk from goats now.'

Turga Galsha, a greying elder of the Hamer, welcomed the author of this book and Jenny Matthews, the photographer, to his hut in Deleme village. Coffee was offered, but first a prayer: for more rain, for the well-being of the guests. All blew a hissing noise, symbolising the breath of life, to close the prayer.

Regular seasons are God's respons-ibility, and the Hamer, scraping by in another year of drought, are fed up with their God. *God has gone to sleep. I've given up begging him,'* says Turga Galsha later. But he stresses that their values remain the same: *'There is no rich person and no poor person among us. Even though God is sleeping, we share everything. This is how we are. Makers of beehives, herders of cattle, and beginners at ploughing.'*

Rastafarianism

Ethiopia is the spiritual home – if not the geographical base – of Rastafarianism, a religious and political movement which began in Jamaica in the 1920s, and has spread throughout the Caribbean, North America, and Western Europe. Hundreds of thousands of people of Afro-Caribbean origin regard Ras Tafari – or the Emperor Haile Selassie, as he later styled himself – as the Messiah and champion of the black race, because he was the king of the only African country never colonised. Rasta-farians, who identify with the Israelites of the Old Testament, await their own 'exodus': redemption for all people of African descent by repatriation back to Africa. Haile Selassie, the Lion of Judah, they believe, is not dead, and one day will lead them home. The most obvious features of Rastafarian culture are their distinctive reggae music and their

'dreadlocks': long braids of hair, often worn under caps in the Ethiopian national colours: red, yellow, and green. But many of them also follow strict dietary laws, and have developed a form of religious mysticism which blends together African and Old Testament practices.

Above: **The Bob Marley Music Shop in Woldiya, Wollo: reggae music comes 'home'.**

Opposite: **A Hamer woman making pottery in the village of Dimeka, south-west Ethiopia**

57

The re-invention of Ethiopia

JENNY MATTHEWS/OXFAM

The last few years of the twentieth century will see the re-birth of Ethiopia, or its return to civil war and despair. A radical policy has been developed to confront the problems of ethnic division which have dogged Ethiopia from its earliest beginnings to the present day. The result, if all goes well, will be a peaceful federation of mutually-dependent states with a good chance of developing and improving the quality of life of their peoples.

Every ethnic group, people, or 'nation' or 'nationality' – the translation of the Amharic word *betsowoch* varies – will, in theory, control its own affairs, in its own language, without interference from outsiders, in a voluntary loose federation administered from Addis Ababa. To avoid the possibility of civil war, every region will even have the right to leave the federation peacefully if it so wishes. This ground-breaking new concept has been described by some as a model for Africa; others regard it as a cynical ploy to stir up trouble among Ethiopia's ethnic groups, and strengthen the power and influence of any one minority ethnic group.

Tribalism used to be a dirty word both for African leaders and for liberal observers of Africa. But it is becoming more and more evident that the nation states into which Africa was divided at independence bear little relation to Africans' actual sense of belonging. Many Ethiopians' first allegiance is to their tribe, or their ethnic group, or their region; their country comes a poor second.

A sense of belonging can be a force for self-reliance. But how will the semi-autonomous regions treat those of mixed blood – those with a mother from Tigray

and a father from Oromia, for example –
or those living outside their 'homeland'?
There are millions of 'mixed' Ethiopians
who may *need* a 'national' identity, and a
national language. A homogeneous
'Ethiopian-ness' *does* exist: in the culture,
family life, and work patterns of most of
Ethiopia. It is needed by Ethiopians
themselves, as a source of pride, identity,
and national cohesion.

Opponents fear that without a sense of
national identity, supported and
encouraged by the central government,
there will be nothing left of Ethiopia in a
few years' time. The centrifugal forces of
ethnic politics may tear the country apart.
Its most vehement critics insist that
ethnic politics is a kind of apartheid.
Pessimists predict that, rather than
breaking new ground, Ethiopia is digging
its own grave.

Supporters of ethnic politics, on the
other hand, argue that this may be the
only way to ensure peace, democracy,
and justice. The risks are great, but it is
undeniable that little progress towards
reconciliation has been made with the aid
of less radical policies in Bosnia, Somalia,
and Rwanda. The Ethiopian experiment
in ethnic politics, if it succeeds, has
implications for many of the racial
disputes that are flaring up in the world
today. For the poor in Ethiopia, the price
of failure will be yet more hardship. In
the words of an African proverb, '*If the
fingers of one hand quarrel, they cannot pick
up the food.*'

MIKE GOLDWATER/OXFAM

D tes and ev nts

1930 Haile Selassie crowned Emperor of Ethiopia.

1935 Italy invades Ethiopia; six years of military occupation follow.

1941 Italians defeated by guerrilla army and Allied troops. Haile Selassie returns from exile.

1962 Eritrea annexed by Haile Selassie, prompting emergence of an Eritrean rebel movement (ELF). Start of civil war.

1972-1974 Famine kills 200,000 Ethiopians.

1973 Eritrean People's Liberation Front (EPLF) formed, superseding ELF.

1974 A group of junior army officers (subsequently known as 'The Derg') overthrow the ageing and unpopular Haile Selassie. Political turmoil ensues.

1975 Rebel movement, the Tigrayan People's Liberation Front (TPLF), emerges in Tigray province.

1977 Lieutenant Colonel Mengistu Haile Mariam emerges as undisputed leader of the Derg regime.

1977-78 Territorial dispute leads to war with Somalia. Ethiopian victory secured with massive support from Russian and Cuban troops. Ethiopia enters Soviet sphere of influence.

1984-85 An estimated half-million Ethiopians die in famine.

1986 Mengistu establishes the People's Democratic Republic of Ethiopia, with a Marxist-Leninist constitution.

1989 Despite forced conscription and military aid from the USSR, the government is driven out of the capital of Tigray province by the TPLF: a turning-point in the 30-year civil war. The rebel coalition EPRDF is formed (the Ethiopian People's Revolutionary Democratic Front: TPLF plus like-minded rebel groups from other regions).

May 1991 Mengistu flees the country before the EPRDF enter Addis Ababa. EPLF enters Asmara and establishes the Provisional Government of Eritrea. In Ethiopia, the EPRDF re-establishes order in the cities, and disarms and disperses the defeated government army.

July 1991 EPRDF invites opposition parties to a national conference on peace and democracy to plan national and regional elections; meanwhile, a transitional government rules. Eritrea is declared free to hold a referendum on independence.

April 1993 98 per cent of Eritreans vote for independence, which is granted.

May 1995 Ethiopian national elections scheduled.

Goats in Jinka market

Update: events in Ethiopia since 1995

Since this book was first published in 1995, Ethiopia has faced many challenges – both internal and external – to its recovery from conflict, chaos, and destitution.

War with Eritrea

Despite the very close historic links between Ethiopia and its neighbour Eritrea – links based on a shared history, a common culture, and vital trade relations – war broke out between the two nations in 1998. The conflict began as a border dispute in May of that year, with Eritrea's occupation of the area around Badme. It turned into a full-scale war which cost an estimated 75,000 lives, displaced more than one million people, and severely damaged the economies of both countries.

Each government has accused the other of territorial aggression and expansionism. The border between the two countries, which was determined in the early years of the twentieth century by the Italian colonial administration, was never demarcated physically on the ground. So the colonial era left a legacy of controversy which soured relations between Eritrea and Ethiopia after independence. However, many observers are convinced that the border issue was only a pretext for the conflict that broke out in 1998. The real problem was an economic one.

Underlying causes of the war

After the downfall of the Derg in Ethiopia in 1991, a bilateral agreement of friendship and co-operation with Eritrea was intended to harmonise the two countries' fiscal, monetary, trade, and investment policies. Ethiopia was able to import and export goods and services through Eritrea's ports, while Eritrea earned about US$ 90 million dollars a year from the provision of services and port duties, and exported a large proportion of its goods and services to Ethiopia. However, this partnership did not last long. After a few years, the two countries were failing to agree on common trade and investment policies. They each introduced separate new investment and tariff regimes, and independent exchange and interest rates. In 1997, Eritrea issued a new currency, the *nakfa,* without due discussion with Ethiopia. The Eritrean government initially assumed that the *nakfa* would be exchanged at parity with the Ethiopian *birr,* and that the two currencies would be usable in both countries. However, the Ethiopian government refused to exchange on the basis of parity, and insisted that all trade and services should now be transacted in hard currency, using a letter-of-credit system. Eritrea rejected this proposal and accused Ethiopia of hostile protectionism. At the same time, Tigray (the northernmost region of Ethiopia, which borders on Eritrea) was developing an industrialisation strategy very similar to that of Eritrea. This was resented by Eritrea, which viewed it as an attempt to undermine its exports into Ethiopian markets.

The human cost of the war

Whatever the causes of the war, the human cost on both sides was devastating. Apart from the estimated 75,000 deaths, tens of thousands of Eritreans and Ethiopians have been expelled from both countries – either for reasons of State security, as the governments claim, or as acts of retaliation. In and near to the battlefields, nearly one million innocent civilians have been displaced. According to the Ethiopian government, 350,000 people had been displaced from the contested area of Badme and Zalanbessa by the end of 1999. The number of displaced Eritreans is likely to be much greater, because the war extended deep inside Eritrea's densely populated areas, with the deployment of more than 400,000 soldiers, fighting with sophisticated modern weapons. Resettlement of displaced people is now an enormously difficult task, and active landmines pose a major threat to reconstruction efforts. Many villages and towns, formerly inhabited by thousands of people, are now devastated beyond the possibility of restoration. In Zalanbessa, for instance, once a town noted for its architectural beauty, around two-thirds of the buildings have been destroyed.

War with Eritrea: 400,000 soldiers, sophisticated modern weapons ... 75,000 people dead and 1,000,000 made homeless

The economic cost

The diversion of their resources to the war has destroyed the efforts of the two governments to reduce the deep and persistent poverty which exists in both countries. Military expenditure rose to 29 per cent of Ethiopia's public spending during the two-year war: more than one million dollars a day.[1] The indirect costs of the war, including the costs incurred as a result of displacement, re-routing the transport of exports and imports, and replacing the assets of the victims, were similarly severe. The international community was reluctant to give assistance to Ethiopia and Eritrea during the war and denied them access to loans or debt-cancellation facilities for more than two years, to put pressure on them to reach a peace agreement. Development assistance was almost frozen as a result.

The political cost

The mutual resentment which has developed between the people of the two countries is one of the most ugly scars left by the war. Their antagonism has been compounded by the communications media of the two countries, and fanned by accusations that the two governments are seeking to destabilise each other, by supporting opposition movements within each other's borders. Ethiopia has accused the Eritrean government of giving military and moral support to the Oromo and Somali opposition groups inside Ethiopia, to increase political instability and insecurity within the country.

The war has aggravated other tensions within Ethiopia, presenting an opportunity for some people to reflect on their grievances against the government, which they perceive to be favouring Tigreans, due to the fact that the administration is dominated by the TPLF (Tigrayan People's Liberation Front).

The war ended in June 2000, when the opposing governments signed a peace proposal sponsored by the Organisation of African Unity. They have generally accepted the judgement of a border-arbitration body. A UN cartographic team has delimited the 1000-km border between them, which is expected to be physically marked on the ground in July 2003. A humanitarian commission established to settle the issues of compensation and other consequences of the war is expected to publish its findings in 2003. But the two govern-ments are still in dispute about the status of Badme, and at present the level of resentment and hostility between them is so great that any attempt to normalise relations between them will be fraught with problems.

The impact on relations with other countries in the Horn

The war between Ethiopia and Eritrea has brought about changes in political alliances in the Horn of Africa.

Somalia

Current relations between the Ethiopian government and the new interim government of Somalia, led by President Abdiqassim Salad Hassan, reflect the history of the relationship between the two countries, which has been characterised by suspicion, conflict, and war. Ethiopia has been reluctant to give official recognition to the new government of Somalia, which took power after Djibouti-hosted peace talks in August 2000. It accuses Somalia of supporting extremist elements, some of which are believed to have links with Islamic fundamentalists and are perceived by Ethiopia as posing a major threat to her national stability. Somalia is also accused of seeking to destabilise Ethiopia by giving support and arms to the Oromo Liberation Front. In return, the Somali interim government alleges that Ethiopia maintains a military presence and political interference in Somalia. Ethiopia denies all the allegations. Whatever the truth of the matter, relations between Somalia and Ethiopia are crucial to national and regional security and stability.

Sudan

A few years ago, there were no diplomatic relations between Ethiopia and Sudan, because the former accused the latter of direct involvement in an attempt in 1994 to assassinate the Egyptian President, Hosni Mubarak. Sudan was also accused of exporting Islamic extremism and supporting Al-Itthad, a Muslim fundamentalist group in Somalia which is suspected of having links with the terrorist organisation al-Qaeda. But the war with Eritrea has changed the political dynamics of the region and, at least for the present, the hostilities between Sudan and Ethiopia are over. The two governments are accelerating the normalisation process by strengthening their diplomatic links and economic co-operation. Sudan Airline has resumed

North Wollo: 1700 metres above sea-level, in a landlocked country where transport routes are tortuous, and ports – whether in Eritrea, Djibouti, or Sudan – are a very long way off.

its weekly flight to Addis Ababa, and Sudan has offered Ethiopia the use of facilities in Port Sudan, although the infrastructure there is poor, and the distance from Ethiopia is great.

The majority of Ethiopia's imports and exports are still handled by the port of Djibouti, despite complaints of poor management and high tariffs there.

Economic development

In 1993, Ethiopia adopted an economic strategy which aimed to increase agricultural productivity, in order to improve food security in the towns and raise the incomes of the smallholder farming population. It also aimed to improve agricultural export earnings and generate income which could be invested in other sectors of the economy. The World Bank and the International Monetary Fund supported Ethiopia's Economic Reform Programme, which was designed to transform the centralised, nationalised economy into a market-led, privatised system.

Large loans from the international community were conditional upon the implementation of a Structural Adjustment Programme which at first seemed to achieve a quick recovery, with a high rate of growth in the gross domestic product (GDP), and stable prices and exchange rates.

In 1997, however, relations between the government of Ethiopia and the IMF deteriorated. The IMF suspended the concessional loan arrangement negotiated under its Enhanced Structural Adjustment Facility (ESAF), on the grounds that Ethiopia had failed to meet some of the conditions which were supposed to reform the financial sector. The IMF's conditions included market-determined rates of interest and exchange; deregulation of fertiliser prices; privatisation of government-owned enterprises; and higher charges for water and electricity. The government negotiated a new agreement in 1998, but in 1999 the IMF declined to extend Ethiopia's access to the second-year concessional fund. This time it gave the reason as the war between Ethiopia and Eritrea. Meanwhile, Ethiopia's access to debt relief under the HIPC (Highly Indebted Poor Countries) initiative was also delayed on the same grounds.

In 2002, the IMF was satisfied with Ethiopia's economic performance, and agreed that the country should have access to a loan of US$ 14 million under the Poverty Reduction Growth Facility programme. So far, Ethiopia has used US$ 77m of the US$ 133m allocated by IMF for its economic reform programme. On the whole, Ethiopia has achieved relative macro-economic stability. GDP growth has remained strong, at an estimated 5 per cent in 2001/02, while inflation is estimated to have fallen from 11 per cent between 1992 and 1995, to zero in 2000.[2] However, Ethiopia's economic growth is far from being sufficient to pay for significant improvements to basic social services and effective measures to reduce poverty. Ethiopia remains one of the poorest countries in the world, according to the UN's Human Development Index.

The challenge of HIV/AIDS

Until very recently, political commitment to deal with the onslaught of AIDS in Ethiopia did not measure up to the extent of the problem. The first evidence of HIV infection was found in 1984, and the first case of AIDS was reported in 1987. The Ministry of Health estimates that so far 1.2 million Ethiopians have died of AIDS-related illness. Government figures suggest that 2.7 million are currently living with HIV, although experts believe that the actual number could be as much as three to five million.[3] Heterosexual transmission is the primary mode by which the disease spreads. Between 10 and 18 per cent of adolescents are estimated to be HIV-positive.[4] Girls typically contract the virus at an earlier age than boys, as a consequence of cultural practices such as early marriage.

The disease is a major threat to the economic survival of Ethiopia. The fact that HIV attacks young adults who are at the peak of their productive potential has many grave implications for families, for communities, and for the whole country. The Central Statistics Authority has estimated that life expectancy may fall from 55 to 42 as a result of AIDS. Many elderly people who themselves need care are having to support their children who are sick with AIDS, and their orphaned grandchildren: an estimated 1,000,000 children have lost their parents as a result of HIV/AIDS.[5] Absenteeism from offices, farms, and factories due to sickness is now a serious problem which affects many households, and severely damages the national economy. The need to provide care for AIDS patients has serious implications for the national health budget. Currently up to 42 per cent of hospital beds are estimated to be occupied by AIDS patients, according to the Ministry of Health.

The government has established a national HIV/AIDS Council, with a secretariat and members drawn from various sections of society. To signal the government's political commitment to tackling the problem, the Council is chaired by the President of Ethiopia himself. Government departments and NGOs are working at both community and national levels, basing their activities on the comprehensive national five-year

Schoolchildren watch a puppet show about HIV/AIDS, performed by a touring group of young volunteers.

RHODRI JONES/OXFAM

Strategic Plan. They operate prevention programmes which promote behavioural change and raise public awareness; through advocacy and education they campaign against stigma and discrimination; and they provide HIV testing and counselling, and safe blood supplies.

Despite all these efforts, there remains a deep-rooted social stigma attached to the disease. Most of the people infected, and their affected families, feel obliged to remain silent about the problem – which drives it further underground. Prevention efforts are made more difficult by traditional and religious attitudes to the use of condoms; by the powerlessness of the majority of girls and women to negotiate safer sex, in a context where they have almost no economic alternative to marriage; by the grinding poverty that compromises the ability of HIV/AIDS patients to live healthily, let alone afford treatment; and by the prevalence of opportunistic diseases such as malaria and tuberculosis, which attack people with depressed immunity.

Agriculture and food security

Agriculture generates around 50 per cent of the GDP of Ethiopia, and around 85 per cent of export earnings. Eighty-five per cent of the population earn their livelihoods through subsistence farming, based on rain-fed food production on smallholdings whose average area is only one hectare. Coffee is the major export crop, constituting one-third of the country's export earnings.

Insecure supply of food is one of Ethiopia's most persistent structural economic problems. It is attributed to a number of daunting factors, including erratic and insufficient rainfalls; high population growth; the fragmentation and degradation of land; the prevalence of pests and diseases; high prices of agricultural inputs; limited access to credit; and improper land management, inadequate farming techniques, and inappropriate policy decisions. A number of policy measures to boost food security and reduce vulnerability have been adopted by the current government, ranging from establishing a national Early Warning System to detect signs of famine, and improving the provision of agricultural extension services, to implementing emergency-preparedness measures. Some of these systems, including the early warning system, have been praised by many commentators as very effective.

As this edition goes to press (May 2003), Ethiopia has once again been hit by a major drought. Fourteen million people are at risk of serious food shortages, three times as many as in the terrible famine of 1984–85.[6] Much of the population is living in a state of constant vulnerability, and there are signs that people are unable to cope with the situation. There are reports of large numbers of cattle dying in the Amhara and Somali regions, with up to 15 per cent of the population suffering from malnutrition in some areas. People's apparently endless resilience in coping with recurrent droughts and hunger is coming under acute strain: repeated poor harvests and the high prevalence of poverty and disease have depleted their resources to dangerous levels.

The impact of AIDS means that this state of affairs can only get worse.

Ogaden, 2000: 'We used to have 200 sheep and 40 cows before the drought. We have just 10 sheep left. My husband doesn't have any work, so he cuts wood to sell, and we use the money for food.'

CRISPIN HUGHES/OXFAM

Experience in Southern Africa shows that ill health among young adults threatens the long-term food supplies of communities who were formerly able to keep going and weather the hard times. The Ethiopian government has appealed for non-food items, including medical supplies and water-supply tools, to the tune of US$ 76 million, but the response of the international community is as yet inadequate.

Land: still a hot issue

Ethiopia has passed through various types of land-administration systems, linked to three different forms of political rule: the monarchy, the socialist era, and the current federal republic. During the monarchy, there was a dual system of land tenure. In the north, where the *rist* system was dominant, a member of a community would claim a portion of the shared agricultural land in the village by proving descent from the village. In the south, the *gult* system was predominant, in which land was given by the Emperor to soldiers and civil servants as a reward for their services. In 1975, at the start of the socialist regime, land was proclaimed to be the property of the State. Farmers had the right to use the land, but all private ownership and transactions in land were outlawed, and the freedom to hire labour was restricted.

After the collapse of socialism, the Constitution of 1995 decreed that land remained in public ownership. Although land-policy reform has since relaxed some of the constraints on use, the sale and purchase of land are still prohibited. The government's view is that any significant changes to land policy require not only the involvement of regional parliaments, but also a change in the federal constitution.

To tackle problems created by shortage of land, redistributions took place in 1991 and 1996–97. The former measure was intended to address the problems of settlement-returnees and ex-soldiers, while the latter was implemented in Amhara region to reverse allegedly uneven patterns of land possession. But in north Wollo zone, for instance, areas of land as small as a quarter of one hectare were allocated to newly married couples and re-settlers, and this policy has been criticised for actually aggravating the fragmentation of land holdings, which all too often leads to the degradation of the land in question. In any case, the redistribution of land alone is no solution to the problem of the lack of land to distribute: in many farming communities, a growing population is claiming an ever-decreasing amount of usable land.

In Ethiopia, whose economy is mainly based on agriculture, the issue of land distribution is obviously highly controversial. The government argues that abolishing State ownership and adopting the freehold system will lead to large-scale landlessness, because many of the peasants would probably be forced by poverty to sell their land to profiteers, which would lead to their eviction and

Northern Wollo: women watering vegetables in a community garden which supports 18 families

RHODRI JONES/OXFAM

forced migration to urban areas, where they would face a very uncertain future of poverty and misery. Critics of the government's policy on rural land tenure believe that the true motive for retaining public ownership is to keep control over the government's constituencies. The system has been much criticised for giving tenants no security, and discouraging the mobility of the rural population, so reducing the size of family holdings and creating further environmental degradation.

In relation to urban areas, government policy has been very different. A system of leasing land in the cities permits leaseholders to sub-let or sell the property on the land, besides extending their leases. The government has argued that the urban land system provides a marketable system of land holding, while retaining the principle of State ownership: in the urban areas, and particularly in Addis Ababa, land for investment can be acquired through auctions, with lease periods ranging from 30 to 99 years. However, many commentators argue that investment is deterred by the high costs of leasing, with heavy down-payments required, and by the lengthy bureaucratic procedures involved.

Political developments

Since the first edition of this book was published, Ethiopia has held two national elections. The first, in 1995, put in place a democratically elected government after four years of rule by a transitional administration, composed of various groupings who had fought to overcome the Derg regime. EPRDF, the major political alliance, won a landslide victory. Almost all the opposition parties boycotted the process. EPRDF was accused of intimidation and vote rigging. The second election was held in May 2000, and was reported by domestic and international observers to be a fair, well-organised, and inclusive process. Although the major opposition groups, including the Ethiopian Democratic

Party, All Amhara People's Organisation, the Oromo Liberation United Front, and the Oromo National Congress, ran for seats, 85 per cent of the House of People's Representatives and the Federal Council remained in the hands of the EPRDF.

In 1995, the Ethiopian federalist structure was installed, with the aim of devolving power to regional administrative structures, formed in the main on the basis of ethnicity and language. The regional governments have extensive economic and political autonomy, although the federal government has influencing power on monetary issues, ownership of land, regulation of foreign trade and investment, and a nation-wide transport policy.

The principle of basing federal and regional administrations on ethno-linguistic factors is a key aspect of the political philosophy of TPLF, the dominant party in the ruling coalition government. This remains a hotly debated issue. The opposition groups argue that such ethnic federalism is a potential threat to the Ethiopian national identity and the nation's sense of shared values. However, others argue that rulers of Ethiopia have tried to build a sense of national identity for centuries, but without much success: most people have remained loyal to their particular ethnic group. Hence, they say, the new system reflects reality. Feelings of national identity and pride have mostly been limited to occasions when Ethiopia as a State has had to defend itself. (The recent war with Eritrea is an obvious example.) The case in favour of ethnic federalism is that Ethiopia is a country which is rich in ethnic diversity but suffers from unequal distribution of power and resources between ethnic groups. Power and authority have in the past been systematically centralised by successive regimes, which have favoured one ethnic group – the Amhara. Devolution of power through the federal system, it is argued, is the sole means of ensuring the equal distribution of political power.

Another challenge facing the government is the internal split within the TPLF. The Front played a crucial role, if not a leading role, in ending the regime of the Derg in 1991. It has also played an influential role in developing the idea of federalism based on ethnicity and language, and it has influenced the implementation of this policy. In short, TPLF, as a major force in the EPRDF, provides an ideological direction to the government of EPRDF. In the past two years, TPLF has been challenged by internal divisions. Its leaders split into two factions over differences in ideology, the war with Eritrea, and the question of corruption within the party and the government. There was some speculation that this would lead to radical political change in Ethiopia, because TPLF is at the centre of Ethiopia's national political dynamic. However, this was not the case. The immediate crisis within the party seems to be over, at least for the time being. Some of the dissidents left Ethiopia as refugees; others were detained on charges of corruption; and another small group apologised and rejoined the party, giving the TPLF leadership the chance to consolidate their ideological position in the party.

Prospects for democracy

The prospects for democracy in Ethiopia are unsure. On the plus side, under the current administration there has been progress towards creating a democratic culture, allowing individuals to express their political opinions through the press, and permitting the political activity of opposition groups. However, the fact remains that there is still a great deal of political intolerance and a lack of openness among political groups. Currently, there is an unresolved argument between the government and the independent press over the proposed press laws, which will regulate the activities of journalists and the circulation of information. Many see this as a signal of political intolerance of dissent. In terms of international

relations, Ethiopia is considered as a country of strategic importance in efforts to combat international terrorism. Hence, relations with countries of the West, including the USA and the UK, seem to be improving, leading to a flow of finance into Ethiopia to support development activities that focus on good governance and the strengthening of civil society. Many feel, however, that such international support for the existing government will ultimately entrench the power and unity of the ruling party.

Abraham Woldegiorgis
(Former Community Development Team Leader, working for Oxfam GB in Delanta, Ethiopia)

Citizens of Ethiopia are gradually gaining the confidence to express their views.

Notes

1. *The World Guide 2003/2004*
2. Ibid.
3. 'The Next Wave of HIV/AIDS: Nigeria, Ethiopia, Russia, India, and China', September 2002, National Intelligence Council-ICA 2002-04D, www.odci.gov/nic
4. Ibid.
5. 'HIV/AIDS in Ethiopia', A USAID Brief, July 2002, www.synergyaids.com
6. Economic Intelligence Unit Report, December 2002

Facts and figures

JENNY MATTHEWS/OXFAM

Population:	66,040,000 (2002); annual increase: 2.9% (1985-2000)
Cities:	Addis Ababa (2.5 million), Dire Dawa (203,000), Harar (94,000)
Land area:	1,000,000 km^2
Life expectancy:	43 years
Infant mortality rate:	117 per 1000
Under-five mortality rate:	174 per 1000
Access to safe drinking water:	24%
Literacy:	male 44%, female 33%
Primary-school enrolment:	male 43%, female 28%
Secondary-school enrolment:	male 14%, female 10%
Human Development Index ranking:	168 (out of 173) (2002)
GNP per capita:	$668
Annual growth of economy:	3%
Public expenditure:	29% to defence, 31% to social services (1999)
Communications:	4 telephone lines per 1000 people
Currency:	Birr; 8.4 birr = US$ 1 (March 2002)
External debt:	$5481 million ($87 per capita)
Debt service:	17% of exports (1999)
Value of exports:	$984 million
Value of imports:	$1961 million

(All figures relate to the year 2000, unless otherwise specified. Sources: United Nations and the World Bank, quoted in *The World Guide 2003/2004*.)

Giant lobelia growing near Dessie

Further reading

Yeraswork Admassie *Twenty Years to Nowhere: Property Rights, Land Management, and Conservation in Ethiopia* (Africa World Press/The Red Sea Press, 2000)

Donald Crummey *Land and Society in the Christian Kingdom of Ethiopia* (James Currey Publications, 2000)

Wendy James et al. *Remapping Ethiopia: Socialism and After* (James Currey Publications, 2002)

Donald N. Levine *Greater Ethiopia: The Evolution of a Multi-ethnic Society*, second edition (University of Chicago Press, 2000)

Harold Marcus *A History of Ethiopia* (University of California Press, 2002)

Nega Mezlekia *Notes from the Hyena's Belly: An Ethiopian Boyhood* (Picador, 2002)

Fasil Nahum *Constitution for a Nation of Nations: The Ethiopian Prospect* (Red Sea Press, 1997)

Tekeste Negash and Kjetil Tronvoll *Brothers at War: Making Sense of the Eritrean–Ethiopian War* (Ohio University Press, 2001)

Richard Pankhurst *The Ethiopians: A History* (Blackwell, 2001)

Wilfred Thesiger *The Danakil Diary: Journeys through Abyssinia, 1930–1934* (Flamingo, 1998)

Kjetil Tronvoll *Ethiopia: A New Start?* (Minority Rights Group International, 2000; text on-line at www.minorityrights.org.uk)

Bahru Zewde *A History of Modern Ethiopia 1855–1991* (James Currey Publications, 2001)

Battery factory, Addis Ababa

Oxfam GB in Ethiopia

Oxfam was one of the first international humanitarian agencies to work in Ethiopia. Its first grant for development work in Ethiopia was made in 1962; an office was opened in Addis Ababa in 1974, in the wake of a major famine. Since then, a broad-based programme of rehabilitation and development work has been built up in the northern, central, and eastern highland regions, in lowland peripheral areas in the east and south-west, and in densely populated areas of the south.

During the 1984/85 famine, Oxfam played a major role in the international relief effort, organising food-distribution and water-supply projects. When the civil war ended in 1991, Oxfam's priorities shifted towards longer-term community-based development work. Staff now support projects to recover and improve exhausted farmland; to conserve water and re-plant forests; and to help marginalised groups, including disabled people and households headed by women, to earn an income. They are helping to revive, repair, and install community water supplies in several areas of Ethiopia, and supporting health programmes which emphasise the welfare of mothers and children, awareness and prevention of HIV/AIDS, and the provision of community-based family-planning services. Local partners are supported to develop their capacity to respond effectively to emergencies at an early stage.

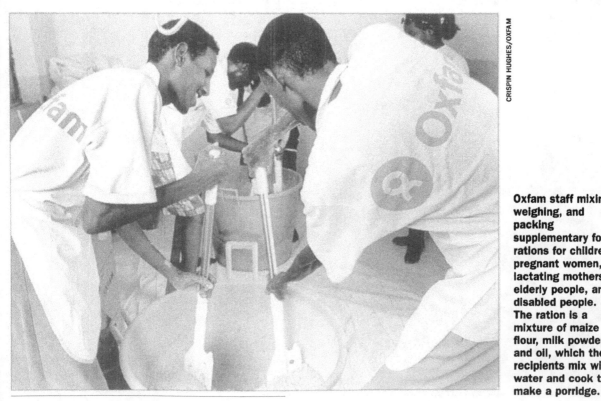

CRISPIN HUGHES/OXFAM

Oxfam staff mixing, weighing, and packing supplementary food rations for children, pregnant women, lactating mothers, elderly people, and disabled people. The ration is a mixture of maize flour, milk powder, and oil, which the recipients mix with water and cook to make a porridge.

Printed in the USA
CPSIA information can be obtained
at www.ICGtesting.com
JSHW060043150824
68134JS00028B/2613